Twayne's United States Authors Series

EDITOR OF THIS VOLUME

Lewis Leary

University of North Carolina

Sylvester Judd

TUSAS 365

Eng.ᵈ by J. Kelnu

In much love,
Your Son. Sylvester.

SYLVESTER JUDD

By FRANCIS B. DEDMOND

Catawba College

TWAYNE PUBLISHERS

A DIVISION OF G. K. HALL & CO., BOSTON

Published in 1980 by Twayne Publishers,
A Division of G. K. Hall & Co.
All Rights Reserved

Printed on permanent/durable acid-free paper and bound
in the United States of America

First Printing

Frontispiece engraving of Sylvester Judd from *Life and Character of the Rev. Sylvester Judd,* ed. Arethusa Hall, 1854.

Library of Congress Cataloging in Publication Data

Dedmond, Francis B
Sylvester Judd.

(Twayne's United States authors series ; TUSAS 365)
Bibliography: p. 154–58.
Includes index.
1. Judd, Sylvester, 1813–1853 —
Criticism and interpretation.
PS2155.Z5D4   818′.409   79-27605
ISBN 0-8057-7305-3

FOR
EADIE

Contents

About the Author

Francis B. Dedmond is Professor of English at Catawba College, Salisbury, N.C. He has published a number of articles on Emerson, Thoreau, and Poe, as well as articles on other nineteenth-century American authors, in such journals as *American Literature, Modern Language Quarterly, Emerson Society Quarterly,* the *Personalist,* and others. Recently he has been engaged in editing the manuscripts of William Ellery Channing the Younger and in preparing an edition of Channing's correspondence to be published by G. K. Hall as an early volume in the American Literary Manuscripts Series, edited by Joel Myerson.

Preface

James Russell Lowell in his *A Fable for Critics* (1848) called Sylvester Judd's *Margaret* "the first Yankee book/With the *soul* of Down East in 't"[1] and implied that with the appearance of Judd on the literary scene American literature stood on the threshold of a new morning. Theodore Parker agreed to send his English friend James Martineau any book published in the United States that he considered to be truly American or truly characteristic of some phase of American life. When Judd's novel *Margaret* was published in 1845, Parker sent Martineau a copy with the assurance that it was "the most truly American book that had been or would be published for some years."[2] Margaret Fuller hailed *Margaret* as a harbinger of what the new literature of America would be like.[3] On April 30, 1846, Emerson was in Cambridge for the inauguration of Edward Everett as President of Harvard. The next day he complained to his journal about the nonliterary character of "these Cambridge feasts" and bemoaned the absence and silence of "the lovers of letters" at the affair. Among the literati Emerson singled out whose voices were not heard was "Judd the author of 'Margaret.' "[4] Yet today specialists in the American literary Renaissance and even students of the Transcendental movement are likely to respond with a "Sylvester who?" when Judd is mentioned.

No writer though ever had a more loving Boswell than Judd had in his adoring aunt Arethusa Hall. And one seeking an answer to the question "Sylvester who?" must start with her *Life and Character of the Rev. Sylvester Judd,* published in 1854. Arethusa, throughout the forty years of Sylvester's life, was successively his nurse, companion of his growing years, most intimate confidante of his formative years, one of his religious converts, an unabashedly affectionate admirer, and his biographer.

In 1811, following the marriage of her sister Apphia to the father of the future novelist, the nine-year-old Arethusa joined the Judd household, where she came, in time, to regard her brother-in-law as her "demi-pere" and where, because of his "imposing presence in the household," she "came to feel for him the affection of the child, the reverence of the teacher, the respect of the man of knowledge, and almost the admiration of the lover."[5] And there is abundant evidence that Miss Hall never lost her "admiration" for the elder Judd.[6]

But her admiration for the younger Judd even more resembled the admiration generally thought to be characteristic of a lover. Sylvester received the full measure of her devotion in life and in death. In 1851, after years of teaching, Miss Hall and Alonzo Gray founded the Brooklyn Heights Seminary in Brooklyn, N.Y., a popular school for girls. In her "Autobiography," Miss Hall wrote:

> The "Life of Sylvester Judd" I . . . wrote while in Brooklyn, taking for it evenings and such other times as I could command outside school engagements. I had known him from birth, had had his confidences and understood his idiosyncrasies, and there seemed to be no one so well qualified to give a true delineation of his character as myself. . . . It was a sad undertaking, but yet a great joy, to have, as it seemed, his living presence with me in going over the review of his whole life, and reproducing its varied scenes from childhood onward; so that at the completion of the work, and the laying aside of all his manuscripts which I had for so long about me, it seemed like losing him afresh. He had been to me more than any other one of my family friends; I received inspiration from him.[7]

The manuscripts Miss Hall mentioned have since disappeared. Yet her biography, which she modestly regarded as a sort of scissors-and-paste compilation in which Judd told his own story, and her other writings about the Judd family, along with the Judd Papers in the Houghton Library of Harvard University and some scattered manuscripts, provide the biographer with the means to answer the question "Sylvester who?"

The purpose of this study, however, is not primarily biographical but analytical and critical. The first two chapters have been devoted to Judd the religious quester and to the man of assurance that he became, not only because he is so little known as to demand a biographical treatment, but also because, as Miss Hall observed, Judd the author was lost in Judd the man and because his works were "intensely the expression of the man."[8]

Preface

Chapter 1 deals with Judd's life through his divinity school days with particular attention to the *sturm und drang* of his spiritual struggles. Chapter 2 deals with the labors of the busy minister, the imaginative efforts of the serious author, the work of the fearless social and political reformer, and the successes of the popular lyceum lecturer.

Miss Hall indicated in the preface to her life of Judd that her intention never was "to enter into any analysis or critical review of his literary productions."[9] In Chapters 3, 4, 5, and 6—each devoted to a separate work—I have attempted what Miss Hall chose not to attempt. Judd's works, however, are not likely to be available to the general reader. In fact, it would be the rare library that would have all of Judd's creative works, especially the first edition of *Margaret,* and the only editions of *Richard Edney* and the dramatic poem *Philo.* I have, therefore, supplied lengthy summaries, along with generous quotations from the works, in the hope that the reader may not only be provided with adequate narrative summaries and a fair rendering of Judd's polemical arguments, but that the reader may also savor something of the flavor, tone, and language of Judd's novels and poetic dramas, and thereby be in a better position to appreciate the critical contentions of the reviewers who reviewed the works at the time of their publication as well as the claims of the critics since.

The concluding chapter—Chapter 7—has a two-fold purpose—to indicate the direction the critical attention given Judd has taken since his death and to determine what Judd's significant contributions were—if any—to the cause of American letters and particularly to the development of the American novel.

FRANCIS B. DEDMOND

Catawba College

Acknowledgments

Until he begins to total up his indebtedness, an author is likely to be unaware how many people, at some point or other, have had a part in his book and how many merit his gratitude. I, in a special way, wish to thank the librarians of the Houghton Library of Harvard University, who, while assisting me in another project but upon learning of my interest in Judd, brought to my attention the mass of uncatalogued Judd Papers in the Houghton. I also wish to thank the librarians who responded so graciously—often even gratis—to my pleas for copies of manuscripts in their collections: John C. Broderick, Chief of the Manuscript Division, Library of Congress; Kenneth A. Lohf, Librarian for Rare Books and Manuscripts, Columbia University; Mrs. Rae R. Brown, Manuscript Assistant, Maine Historical Society; Marc Gallicchio, Manuscript Division, Historical Society of Pennsylvania; Robert A. McCown, Manuscripts Librarian, University of Iowa; Archie Motley, Curator of Manuscripts, Chicago Historical Society; and the Manuscripts Librarians of the University of Virginia, Yale University, and the Massachusetts Historical Society.

I am also grateful to the number of librarians who responded, in one way or another, to my inquiries: Frederick E. Bauer, Jr., Associate Librarian, American Antiquarian Society; Ms. Barbara Crosby, Lithgow Public Library, Augusta, Maine; Philip N. Cronenwett, Curator, Special Collections, The Jones Library, Amherst, Massachusetts; Blaise Bisaillon, Reference Librarian, Forbes Library, Northampton, Massachusetts; and Eric S. Flower, Head, Special Collections Department, University of Maine Library.

To anyone working in the provinces, away from the research centers, interlibrary loan librarians are invaluable angels. I am especially grateful to two: Mrs. Jacquelyn E. Sims of Catawba College and Mrs. Allen Antone of Appalachian State University.

I also want to express my appreciation to Catawba College for awarding me a summer 1978 research grant to help me get out of the provinces, to Mrs. Arlene W. Schenk for carefully preparing a typescript of this book from an often messy handwritten manuscript, to Professor Joel Myerson of the University of South Carolina for making available to me valuable books from his personal collection, and to Professor Richard D. Hathaway, State University College, New Paltz, N. Y., for permission to borrow from his dissertation material in the Judd Papers at the Houghton Library—papers to which he has exclusive access.

And I acknowledge with thanks the permission of the following institutions to quote from letters and manuscripts in their possession: Houghton Library, Harvard University; the University of Iowa; the Massachusetts Historical Society; and the University of Virginia.

Chronology

1813   July 23. Sylvester Judd born in Westhampton, Massachusetts, the second son of Sylvester Judd II and Apphia Hall Judd.

1822   March 29. The elder Judd purchased the *Hampshire Gazette*, published in Northampton, and on May 23 moved his family to Northampton.

1826   Experienced a religious conversion and determined to enter the Orthodox (Calvinistic) Christian ministry.

1831–
1832   Prepared for college at Hopkins Academy, Hadley, Massachusetts. Delivered the valedictory at the graduation exercises.

1832–
1836   Entered Yale College to prepare for the ministry, but became increasingly disturbed by the cardinal doctrines of Calvinism. Graduated Phi Beta Kappa.

1836–
1837   Master of a private school in Templeton, Massachusetts. Converted to Unitarianism.

1837   Summer. Wrote "Cardiagraphy," his religious *apologia*. August 27. Entered the Harvard Divinity School four days before Emerson delivered his Phi Beta Kappa address—"The American Scholar"—in Cambridge.

1838   March. The American Unitarian Association published *A Young Man's Account of His Conversion from Calvinism. A Statement of Facts.*

1839   September. Jones Very shunned Judd's offer of friendship. Reviewed Very's *Essays and Poems* (1839).

1840   July. Graduated from divinity school and began supplying the pulpit of the Unitarian Church in Augusta, Maine. Settled over the church in Augusta. October 1. Frederic Henry Hedge preached the ordination sermon.

1841   August 31. Married Jane Elizabeth Williams of Augusta, daughter of United States Senator Reuel Williams.

1842   January. Appointed Chaplain of both Houses of the Maine Legislature. March 13. Delivered a discourse from his pulpit entitled *A Moral Review of the Revolutionary War* that offended the legislators. March 14. Dismissed as Chaplain.

1844   January. Reinstated as Chaplain. March 22. Completed manuscript of *Margaret.*

1845   February 2. Preached and later published *A Discourse Touching the Cause and Remedies of Intemperance.* August. *Margaret* published by Jordan and Wiley of Boston in an edition of one thousand copies.

1848   Completed the writing of *Philo: An Evangeliad.*

1850   *Philo: An Evangeliad* published (copyrighted December 28, 1849) by Phillips, Sampson and Company of Boston. May 26. Preached on and later published *The True Dignity of Politics. Richard Edney and the Governor's Family* published by Phillips, Sampson and Company.

1851   Revised edition of *Margaret* in two volumes published by Phillips, Sampson and Company. September. Began work on *The White Hills, An American Tragedy.* Left in manuscript at his death. December 31. Granted Felix O. C. Darley permission to prepare an illustrated *Compositions in Outline . . . from Judd's Margaret.* Actually published in 1856.

1853   January 26. Died in Augusta. *The Birthright Church: A Discourse . . . Designed for "Thursday Lecture" in Boston, Jan. 6, 1853* published posthumously.

1854   *The Church: In a Series of Discourses* published posthumously.

CHAPTER 1

Years of Crisis

WITH Sylvester Judd, religion was an ever-present reality. It provided the compelling motivation of his life from early childhood until his death at age forty. As Arethusa Hall put it, "Religion was to him the first thing and the last; . . . it was to him all in all."[1] Yet he was beset by spiritual crisis after spiritual crisis on his pilgrim's progress to religious assurance and certainty. He *must* possess aright that which he was possessed by, and that quest took him through many trials and tribulations and through many a slough of despond on his way to what his friend Jones Very came to regard as the dominant in his character—his assurance of heaven's benediction on him and his calling.

I *Antecedents*

Sylvester Judd—third to bear the name—was born in Westhampton, Massachusetts, on July 23, 1813. The thirty-year-old Jonathan Edwards preached the ordination sermon when Judd's great-grandfather, the twenty-four-year-old Jonathan Judd (1719–1803), was ordained into the ministry on June 8, 1743, and settled over the "Church of Christ in the New Precinct at Northampton,"[2] a parish he served for sixty years. The novelist's grandfather and the first Sylvester (1752–1832) did not follow his father into the ministry, but during the Revolutionary War served as purchasing agent for the Continental Army and, after the war, as a member of the 1779 convention for framing a Constitution for Massachusetts. In time, he became a successful farmer, the part-owner of a general store in the center of Westhampton, the first justice of the peace of the village, and the representative from Westhampton at the General Court in Boston.

Sylvester Judd (1789–1860), the father of the novelist, was essentially a self-educated man whose main scholarly attainments were the result of determination and hard work. At the age of thirteen, having finished his common-school education, he became a clerk in his father's store; but after two years, weary of the confinement and with characteristic boyish restlessness to see something of the world, he went to Boston for six months, where "he fell in with some persons of intelligence, whose influence was to stimulate his own mind to an appreciation of knowledge and a determination for its attainment."[3]

By the time he returned to Westhampton and the store, his determination had become an obsession. What money he could scrape together went for books. Often his reading and study went on into the wee hours of the morning; he needed knowledge, wisdom, and the answers that these would offer to the compelling questions of life. In 1808, at the age of nineteen, he confessed to his journal in an entry that could well have been written by his son Sylvester at the same age:

I have read more religious books this year than I had done any preceding year, paid attention to the arguments for and against the Holy Scriptures, paid some attention to the history of the church, etc. I searched for myself, without paying any regard to my youthful prejudices, and was satisfied of the validity of the Scriptures. . . . I was educated, as I said before, and taught to believe the Christian Religion; taught to believe that the Federalists were right, etc. But when I threw off what I please to call the parental *yoke*, I also, in a great measure, discarded the doctrines in which I had been educated, and was advancing into the regions of chaos and confusion. I was seriously inclined to question the validity of divine revelation, and disposed to embrace the demoralizing principles of Democracy. My mind was in a sort of equilibrium, doubting which way to go. While I was in this state of mental suspense, I determined to study into the principle of human nature, to penetrate into the causes and effects of actions, and weigh with impartiality the *pros* and *cons.* I determined to let my own reason be the criterion, and not another man's.[4]

This year, 1808, was, the young clerk confessed, the most important year of his life—the year of his reformation, the year of more "efficient progress in knowledge . . . than any former year," having gone that year through navigation, algebra, and mathematics in general and having given, along the way, some attention to astronomy and the geography of the world. "I read," he noted, "Gibbon's History of Rome, without imbibing his infidelity. I paid some attention to the theory of Government; more especially of the American Constitution. I observed the cause of the rise, progress and decline of nations, etc. I studied much as possible into science in general, endeavoring to reason and act for myself, and to form opinions of my own. But my judgment is yet immature, and my ideas crude and undigested."[5]

Later, as his journal entries show, he tackled the French language, gaining "by unwearied assiduity" a "tolerably good knowledge of it."[6] "Had I time," he wrote, "I could obtain a competent knowledge of Latin, but *tempus deest mihi.*"[7] He did, however, master Latin sufficiently well to read Virgil and progressed far enough into biblical Greek to be able to read the New Testament in the original language.

In October 1810 the twenty-one-year-old clerk entered into partnership with his father and others in the establishment of the firm of Judd, Hooker & Co., a mercantile firm operating in Northampton, Westhampton, and Norwich, Massachusetts. Business was good, and the young scholar-merchant felt that he was now in a position to take on added responsibility. On January 16, 1811, he married Apphia Hall of Norwich, whose father, Aaron Hall, left Harvard in his freshman year to join the Revolutionary forces and who, at a ripe old age, delighted in telling stories of the times that tried men's souls to the listening ears of delighted grandchildren. Like Sylvester's paternal grandfather, Squire Hall too was a justice of the peace and a representative in the General Court.

Although family responsibilities cut into his study time, his desire for knowledge continued to increase. His business prospered; and, as he put it, "I did not apprehend that I could possibly meet with severe losses, or find much difficulty in getting a livelihood."[8] So, shortly after the birth of Sylvester in 1813, the young merchant built a spacious house for his bride and growing family near the Westhampton store, planted it about with an orchard, shade trees, and flowering shrubs, and moved his family from the rented house where James W., the first child, and Sylvester were born. Three other sons—Chauncey Parkman, Hall, and Hophni—followed in rapid succession, all born in the "new house," as it was called.

In February 1815 peace was concluded with England following the War of 1812. Excited by the economic prospects peace promised, the ambitious merchant "formed a plan of going on with trade with life and vigor, alone."[9] He borrowed money, went to Hartford, Providence, Boston, and New York, and bought large quantities of goods. But prices declined, and the merchant lost four hundred dollars the first year. Again, he entered into a partnership, turned his attention to farming, and in 1818 entered the tanning business. But things went from bad to worse, and he complained to his journal:

1819. I have come to another year, which forms a grand era of my life. In April, I dissolved with friend Hooker, and again undertook business alone. I entered more largely into the tanning business, but did less farming than before. I found myself $600 or $700 in the rear, and determined to make one desperate effort to better my affairs. I purchased goods and hides largely, and involved myself in debt to the amount of about $8000! little imagining the turn of times which was before me. The year 1819 is the year in which the full effects of peace in Europe and this country were realized here, as well as the effects of our former extravagance and improvidence. There was a great depreciation of all kinds of property, real and personal, a general stagnation of business, no money in circulation, many failures, and universal distrust,—no foreign markets, no profitable navigation. With this great amount of property on hand, and debts on my shoulders, I was cast upon these trying times.[10]

These trying times left the merchant depressed as bankruptcy threatened. He needed a change of scenery, he felt; he "resolved to leave scenes where nothing was calculated to soothe and alleviate, but everything excited feelings of discontent, of pain and anguish." He felt he might "be obliged to seek a refuge in the western wilderness"[11] for himself and his family. In fact, on September 13, 1819, he left his wife and sons and went on a nine-week trip through New York to Ohio. Disappointed with what he found there, he returned to Westhampton on November 20, determined to turn every stone in order to collect money for his creditors. All that he had worked for had ended in disappointment, loss, and vexation.[12]

How much the fact of a missing father disturbed the sensitive, impressionable Sylvester, we can only guess. He might have been too young to appreciate the straitened financial circumstances of the family, but he was surely aware of the dejected mood of his father—a dejection that only increased with time. In a journal entry, dated August 21, 1821, the distraught family man wrote: "I am now quite hoary-headed, considerably deaf with one ear, infirm in bodily health, my brow beginning to wrinkle with care, and what is more important, my mind is broken with trouble and losses, its energy gone, with no resolution to go forward, and no patience to remain as I am."[13] In taking stock of himself, he noted that he had lost the judgment, industry, and penetration requisite for money-making. "The gilded hopes of youth," he wrote, "the projects of ambition, the impatience of disappointment, the allurements of future life, *these, these* things have left me. Poverty and obscurity have lost half their terrors. Indeed, they sometimes appear pleasing. . . . Instead of being a statesman, I am willing to be a shepherd. How long I shall be of this opinion, I know not. I am liable to change. Extremes are my characteristics."[14]

A chance to change soon came. On March 29, 1822, the elder Judd purchased the *Hampshire Gazette,* published in nearby Northampton. His brother Hophni, at the time of his death on March 15, 1818, was editor of the *Gazette* and one-fourth owner of the newspaper. After his death, Hophni's share continued to be held by his father. We wonder how the financially harassed family man raised the necessary capital; yet he recorded in his journal that he "purchased the other three-quarters, determined to make one more effort to live in the world."[15] He assumed the editorship of the *Gazette* in April, and on May 23 he moved his family to Northampton.

II *Childhood in Northampton*

Northampton was a beautiful village. Its streets were lined with wide-spreading, venerable elms, and the village was famous for its well-kept gardens. Nearby was Round Hill with its wooded summit, looking out over green fields, rich meadows, and neat little villages. Stretching off in the distance, with the irregular peaks of Holyoke and Tom in the foreground, were the mountains.

These appealing scenes of his early boyhood made a deep yet disturbing impression on the mind and the spirit of the growing Sylvester, for his love of the beauty of nature clashed with his developing religious devotion. Years later in reminiscing about his boyhood, he wrote of his struggle in a manner that betrays his instinctive Transcendental leanings:

Religion, which as a subject of thought often engaged my attention, and as a subject of feeling deeply interested my heart, was a mystery to me. . . . I can but allude to the irrepressible desire, the craving of my heart, for a full participation in the religious feeling. But the influences of my creed came over my spirit like an autumnal frost, and sealed up the fountains of emotion. Abused Nature did not always remain silent under her injuries. She poured her complaints into my ears with a voice that I should not have disregarded. . . .

The works of God were all perverted to me. They were dispossessed of their highest, their religious beauty. When I fished by the river side, when I rambled in the woods, when my fancy led me to a favorite hill-top that overhangs as lovely a landscape as our continent embraces, I thought this world is beautiful; I thought it beneficient in its uses; I felt that there was a unison between the scene around me and my own heart. But then I knew that my nature was cursed; and I supposed that this harmony was depraved, or at least that there was nothing desirable about it; and I did not allow myself to cherish it as much as I wished, nor with that delight which it has since afforded me. I used to repine almost, that I had not lived with Adam in Paradise, when the earth was *really* beautiful, and man's nature could properly sympathize with its charms. I used to hope that I might live to see the millennium, when this double curse would be removed, and man would be restored to the true enjoyment of nature. I looked up at the stars at night: I supposed that they had been cursed. While my imagination would be revelling in the idea of their number and distances, my heart would throw itself abroad, and mingle somewhat in spirituality with the infinite God who made them; I felt something of humility, something of adoration, something of love; — but I had not been converted. Of course my feelings were not religious. There could be no right harmony between my heart and the unsullied glories of God's handywork, which thronged the firmament.[16]

More than anything else, then, the schoolboy longed for religious conversion. With a mind and heart so naturally susceptible to religious impressions and with his unusual concern for his spiritual welfare, thirteen-year-old Sylvester was ready for the religious revival that came to Northampton in 1826. "Into its scenes of stirring interest and solemn devotion," he later wrote, "I entered, with that enthusiasm which the subject was adapted to enlist, and which my own nature prompted. I found that which I sought. I was happy in the free exercise of a new heart, and was satisfied in my election being secure."[17] So eager was he to let others know of the great things that had come to him and so concerned was he for the salvation of his companions that he held religious meetings in barns where, mounted on a barrel's head, he would put forth earnest appeals to his playmates to forsake sin and enter the pathway of eternal life.

III *Frustrated Youth*

Perhaps it was Sylvester's religious conversion that intensified his desire to further his education. Now that heaven was sure, he no doubt wanted to give himself in service to God and his fellowman. But the prospects seemed dim that he would be able to prepare himself for college, much less be able to get a college education. The *Hampshire Gazette* was prospering under his father's editorial guidance; subscriptions had doubled; but the editor was not one to press his subscribers or debtors, and his income, in reality, was hardly sufficient to support his ever-increasing family and to make the payments that honor demanded on the Westhampton debts.

Thus, in 1828, with his common-school education behind him and the prospects of further education bleak, Sylvester became increasingly sullen and depressed. He talked of going to sea, and some of his friends were convinced that he was utterly serious. Some months were spent with his grandfather Judd, who had been left behind in Westhampton when the family moved to Northampton; and there, amid scenes of his childhood, Sylvester became somewhat reconciled to the inevitable: he must go to work.

Like his father before him, he turned to the mercantile business. For six months in the spring of 1829, Sylvester worked as a clerk in the store of an uncle in Greenfield, Massachusetts, moving on later to Hartford, Connecticut, where he was also employed as a dry-goods clerk. But he was soon dismissed from the Hartford job. "An indelible stigma is fixed upon my character," he wrote his father from Hartford on October 14, 1830, "at least so far as concerns my capacity of remaining a merchant's clerk. I know not what to do." With New York so near, he might, he said, sign on a ship in some capacity or other, "and sail for distant climes, where neither the queries of *present* friends, the inquiries of *present* relations, nor the sneers of *present* enemies, will trouble me more." Realizing, though, that such a life was not for him, he pled in near desperation, "Still I hope it is not now too late to appeal to the heart of a father." The boy then reminded his father of what he remembered reading earlier in his father's journal: "'I ought to have been sent to college, a place by far best calculated to develop the natural propensities of my mind.'" Sylvester then concluded: "If I know anything of myself, I think I can say without self-flattery, that such is my own case, using the present for past time. Do I appeal in vain, when I ask, in short, that I may have a *liberal* education?"[18]

IV   Hopkins Academy

The boy's plea apparently struck home, for his father arranged for him to spend the winter of 1830–31 with his grandfather Judd in order that he might attend Dr. Wheeler's school in Westhampton. When he returned to Northampton in the spring, his father agreed to enroll him in the Hopkins Academy at Hadley, three miles away. Sylvester was to board at home and walk the daily six-mile round trip; the family coffers would be strained, therefore, only for the tuition. Sylvester was warned not to take the opportunity to prepare for college as any assurance that college was more than a very doubtful possibility.

Nevertheless, he threw himself with abandon into the study of Greek, Latin, and mathematics and showed in his student essays his early interest in moral and religious questions. In his second year, he tried his hand at poetry, addressing one of his poems to "Poverty," showing, as Arethusa Hall says, "his sense of the pecuniary embarrassments which hindered the gratification of his wishes":

> Thou Potent one, in strongest chains
> Who bind'st me filled with woes and pains,
> Do break the rivet, set me free.
> ....
> . . . no good, I'm sure
> To hold me thus. It will not cure
> My restlessness, however tight
> Thou fitt'st these manacles.
> ....

Good sir, loose, loose your hold.
Where science leads, I wish to go,
And soon to reach Fame's temple too;
Where mind's choice pleasures grow,
I wish to tread, and there to sow
The seeds of influence and esteem.[19]

Yet, despite all, his years at Hadley were successful and satisfying ones; and in August 1832, at the end of his second and final year at Hopkins Academy, Sylvester delivered the valedictory address.

However, during the two-year period preceding his days at Hopkins—the years of frustration—his religious faith had been sorely tried; he thought even of giving it up completely. But with the chance to prepare himself for college, his natural boyish exuberance returned. He united with the Calvinistic church in Northampton and determined to enter the Orthodox Christian ministry. And when, in the midst of his Hopkins Academy days, another revival came to Northampton, he, "burning with the desire that all might be saved, and filled with horror at the thought of the eternal misery of any soul, . . . with other young converts of the time, labored, in season and out of season, for the conversion of the impenitent, and for the arousing of the old professing Christians, who, it seemed to them, were dead to the tremendous realities of their obligations."[20] Sylvester and a companion even embarked on a missionary tour through the neighboring towns.

V   *Yale*

In 1832 Sylvester entered Yale College at New Haven, at the time a bastion of Orthodoxy. To continue his education was now imperative if he were to prepare for the ministry. His father promised to do what he could to help; the hope was that Sylvester could do some teaching or work at odd jobs during the vacations. On September 27 the young ministerial student noted in his journal: "On Tuesday last, I was examined, and admitted Freshman here. I begun a new life."[21] A serious student from the beginning, he did not find his studies to be of "a nature to weary the spirit with constant tediousness and difficulty. Devotion to them," he wrote his parents, "may be a recreation rather than a task."[22]

Late in January 1833 he entered in his journal a lengthy statement which he entitled "Consecration." Following a preface in which he confessed his weakness, sinfulness, and proneness to go astray when subjected to the temptations of the world, the flesh, and the devil, he consecrated himself with all his time, talents, influence, thoughts, property, and knowledge to God and his service. "I make a dedication of my ALL," he wrote. "Henceforth, fare thee well, vain world! Welcome, Cross! I'll take thee up, and bear thee through strife, through sneers, though death be my portion. . . . This act of consecration is to be in force to-day, to-morrow, next year, while I live, in death, and after death—*to all eternity*. I henceforth . . . stand before the world a *Christian;* a stranger and sojourner here; as one who is not of this world, but as one whose heart and treasure are laid up in heaven."[23]

Throughout his first year at Yale, Sylvester's letters to his family seemed to be principally directed at urging them to give care to their spiritual well-being. However, to his favorite aunt and confidante, Arethusa Hall, he admitted to some urgings and promptings of his earthly nature. He could, he wrote, become "half enticed" by Horace's sensuality or "wrapt in the story of Helen and Priam." "Love!" he continued, "how strange a thing it is! As you remarked going to B., it rules the world. Yes, little naked Cupid, with his bow and arrow, effects a mightier conquest than all the crested myriads of ancient times, or all the artillery of modern days." He concluded, "If I don't get me engaged first, I want you to select for me the most suitable of your heaven-born pupils. The wife makes the man. If you make the wife, you may make me. So don't despair yet."[24]

In his second year at Yale, Sylvester became increasingly disturbed by the Calvinistic doctrines he had so wholeheartedly embraced. He was going through yet another spiritual crisis. His letters to his family contained veiled hints that all was not well, but he resolved to keep the depth of his tortured feelings to himself. In his junior year, he became unusually reserved and wrote less frequently to family and friends. Early in his senior year, he wrote his mother that, given what he had been through, nothing could induce him to repeat his college days. He confided to a sister-in-law, "When I contemplate writing you, I feel that I must unlock the secret chambers of my soul, and present to you a transcript of what passes therein. This I *cannot do*. It would do you no good, nor will it benefit me. Everyone possesses his own secrets, which he keeps concealed in his own bosom, revealing them to no mortal eye."[25] He wrote his brother Hall that his odd and low-spirited behavior during the spring vacation was brought on as a result of *"a religious affair."* [26]

While Sylvester in New Haven wrestled with his spiritual crisis, his father back home wrestled with a personal and political crisis of his own. The elder Judd was nominally a Whig, and the *Gazette* was regarded generally as a Whig paper; but in the midst of the intense party strife generated by the election of Andrew Jackson, the editor lapsed from the expected ideological purity. On September 17, 1834, he wrote in his journal: "I am assailed because I said something in the paper favorable to the working-men. The spirit of aristocracy belongs to human nature. . . ."[27] And following a Whig convention in October, he wrote: "There is no honesty in the politics of this country, none in electioneering. It is all trickery and management."[28] On October 19, he noted in his journal: "I am suspected of Jacksonianism, and all other isms, because I do not choose to put on the Whig collar and do their dirty work."[29] After the Whig sweep of Massachusetts in November, the suspicion was raised to a finger-pointing cry of Jacksonianism against the hapless editor.

The Jackson men, sensing that a fellow traveler may be in their midst, attempted to enlist the elder Judd and his paper in their cause. But he had had his fill; he accepted an offer of two thousand dollars for the *Gazette* and, on December 30, "bid adieu" to his readers. He had had enough of the world of business. He would live "in a humble way, upon such means as he had, thus leaving himself free for such mental occupations as he might be drawn to. . . ."[30] He turned to genealogical, historical, and antiquarian research and writing, which, however, did not preclude his engaging in the reform movements of the day. By late 1835 he was active in the cause of abolitionism,[31] as much so, perhaps, as he had earlier been in the temperance movement. But what all this meant to the twenty-two-year-old Sylvester was that, from his father, he could now expect even less financial support than before. Yet a half dozen years later, he would benefit, in a literary way, when he turned to his father for aid in securing background information and local color for *Margaret*.

VI   *Conversion to Unitarianism*

Despite his problems—the ubiquitous financial one and the debilitating religious one—Sylvester graduated Phi Beta Kappa from Yale in 1836 and, in the fall, became master of a private school in Templeton, Massachusetts, determined to pay off his college debts, a burden he now must assume alone. There in Templeton, for the first time in his life, he found himself in close daily contact with Unitarians, the enemies of Calvinistic orthodoxy; but to his surprise, he found many of the Unitarian views remarkably similar to some of the heretical notions that had disturbed him so deeply. Here he was in the enemy camp, he who had consecrated himself to the Orthodox ministry; he *must not* allow himself to be religiously seduced. And yet. . . .

By early spring 1837 his conversion to Unitarianism was virtually complete. From Templeton on March 24 he wrote to his brother James that he could no longer accept the Calvinistic doctrine of depravity. "A spiritual nature," he asserted, "was given us, by which to mount up, as on eagle's wings, to an elevated existence, to an assimilation with the Deity."[32] Sylvester anticipated that persecution would come with his changed views. "Let persecution come," he wrote. "Only let *truth*, God's own truth, prevail. I anticipate the day when truth shall ride forth, conquering and to conquer."[33] The Lord had worked in mysterious ways, plunging him into dark despair, making him wretched in the struggle, and haunting him with the bitterest agony of all— the utter disappointment he knew his defection would be to his dearest and closest friends. But God had—and would—sustain him, and he was now resolved. The first test of his determination came when he was offered an attractive teaching job at Miami College, which he labeled "an Old School Presbyterian College in Ohio."[34] He rejected the offer.

Yet six weeks later, still prolonging the struggle, still delaying a clean break, Sylvester wrote in his journal: "Go to the Unitarian Church. Oh! tis misery to think of it. It is an *open* step, which I have not yet taken. Truth, thy way is a thorny one. . . ."[35] He was sure his friends would rather see him in his grave; and by late June he was sunk again in deep despair, in yet another slough of despond. He moaned: "My spirits are gone, my vigor, my ambition. What will raise me, I know not. The future is one black atmosphere of night. Its heavy darkness is reflected upon the present."[36] Nothing, he soon concluded, would raise him up except an open embracing of Unitarianism and a reasoned declaration on his part to his family of the faith that was in him.

By the end of June 1837 he was back home in Northampton; and he began his *apologia,* which he entitled "Cardiagraphy." His was a delicate, painful task. Admitting openly that he had changed "so far as relates to the fundamental points of all religion,"[37] he asserted though that he himself had, in reality, undergone no conscious change: the goal of his life was still God's glory and man's happiness. After reviewing the religious affections and susceptibilities that had been his since early childhood, he declared these feelings—these holy and delightful emotions—to be as dear to him as ever. Now, however, they rested on the inner, incontrovertible evidence of consciousness, which he referred to as "the eye of the soul."[38] His very nature, he argued, demanded that he rely upon the perceptions of his soul-consciousness, upon intuitive perceptions. He must discover the laws of his own nature if he would discover the laws of God. Once he discovered them, his obligation would be then, as Emerson would later maintain in "Self-Reliance," to obey them, knowing that they would never be contrary to his consciousness, to his nature, nor to his reason. Whether or not Judd read Emerson's *Nature* during his sojourn among the Unitarians at Templeton is not known, but his personal narrative sets forth views remarkably akin to some of the cardinal ones in Emerson's little book.

In "Cardiagraphy," Judd pictured himself as now no longer in "the abyss of doubt and universal scepticism."[39] He had, he said, from early childhood been taught that Calvinism was assuredly the religion of the Bible, a reasoned conclusion his father came to in his own *annus mirabilis* before Sylvester's birth. Yet even as a child, his original nature had "uttered its stern notes of remonstrance and reprehension at my self-immolation on the altar of prescription."[40] Ultimately, his original nature won out; but in the process he, at times, felt that he was losing his Bible, his religion, and his God. He clung, however, to his Bible; in nature he found anew the Creator; and religion was restored to him.

But this religion rejected the cardinal doctrine of original sin— the doctrine of native defilement—on which most of the other objectionable doctrines of Calvinism were based. He now saw all

God's creation—including man—as good. In fact, all creation conspired to the happiness of man and to the glory of God. The chief work, however, of the Almighty was the breathing into man of the breath of life—the creation of the soul. However, the doctrine of total depravity, the handmaiden of the doctrine of original sin, decreed, Judd declared, that man in his soul must hate all good, including God. Man, in Judd's view, though, was created in God's image to love him and to love all things lovely. "To know ourselves," he wrote, "and not act according to our nature, is supreme folly and unhappiness. To know ourselves, and yet willingly debase our natures, is rebellion against our Maker, and justly exposes us to his wrath."[41] When man finds in himself the image of God, only then can he form a true idea of his own dignity. Religion is the soul's love of God.

These views were true, Judd was convinced, else there was neither God, religion, nor the soul. Reason, the arbiter of the soul, guided the seeker to the very throne of God, where he discovered that love was the fulfilling of the law. Rejecting the charge that Unitarianism was cool toward God and man, but admitting the "odor" associated with the name even among members of his own family, he concluded:

If to desire the greatest happiness of the universe, and the highest glory of God; if to see the wisdom and goodness of God displayed in *all* his works; if to take elevated views of his noblest work, man; if to believe and love the revelation which God has made of himself to man; if to unite the philosopher and the Christian, and make them harmoniously subserve the same chief end; if to desire to see the image of God, wherever prostrate, raised,—wherever bright, made still more radiant; if, in a word, to desire to see man illuminated in his darkness, purified from his sins, delivered from the dominion of his Adversary, elevated from his degradation, and to see him loving and being loved, ascending toward his God, unfolding his large capacities for the bliss and holiness of the skies; rising, in the full vigor of his strength, in the intensity of his longings, upward and upward, till earth and heaven shall meet in rapturous unison; and the souls of men and angels, and the Spirit of the living God, shall flow together in one infinite, changeless heart of love;—I say, if this is to be a Unitarian, then I am one.[42]

VII   *At Harvard Divinity School: Emerson*

With the cool acquiescence of his family and with his physical and psychic health impaired by his recent struggle, Judd entered the Harvard Divinity School in late August 1837. Four days after his arrival in Cambridge, Emerson delivered his lecture "The American Scholar" before the Phi Beta Kappa society. Judd was a Yale Phi Beta Kappa, and some echoes of Emerson's address in subsequent letters Judd wrote would indicate that Judd heard the Concord Transcendentalist in person. For instance, Emerson proclaimed that ". . . if the single man plant himself indomitably on his instincts, and there abide, the huge world will come round to him."[43] On September 7—a week after Emerson's address—Judd wrote to his favorite aunt and future biographer, "If we stand still, *I have heard it said*, the world will come round to us."[44]

In his address, Emerson singled out nature as the main influence on the human mind, particularly on the mind of the scholar. "There is never a beginning, there is never an end, to the inexplicable continuity of this web of God, but always circular power, returning to itself. Therein it resembles his own spirit, whose beginning, whose ending, he never can find,—so entire, so boundless. . . . Nature hastens to render account of herself to the mind."[45] Writing to his mother on September 7, Judd declared, ". . . We can commune with ourselves and our God. And we can hold converse with nature, who is never engaged, but always solicits our acquaintance by innumerable attractions. We need never *fear* to make the acquaintance of nature. Man sometimes deceives us; nature, never. . . . She is my companion, my study, my delight. She reveals a God."[46]

Emerson said, "The world,—this shadow of the soul, or *other me*,—lies wide around. Its attractions are the keys which unlock my thoughts and make me acquainted with myself."[47] In something approaching a paraphrase of Emerson's statement, Judd, in commenting to his mother on one like himself who spent his time under the stars, said, "He pours out his heart into the ear of nature, and he would listen to her response. She becomes at once his confidante and his oracle."[48] Other echoes could be cited, but of more significance than the echoes is the evidence that Judd, at the time of his entrance into the Divinity School, was receptive to some of the basic Emersonian views.

Judd had other opportunities to hear Emerson lecture during his first year at Harvard. Even if he heard none of the lectures in Emerson's 1837–38 Boston series on "Human Culture," Judd—as he might well have done—could have heard Emerson repeat three of the lectures in Cambridge in the early spring. On March 8, 1838, in his lecture on "The Heart," Emerson dealt with a problem that was then disturbing Judd; Judd needed a close and sympathetic friend. Emerson said that the soul longs for the society of and oneness with a noble mind. But the perfect friendship requires natures so rare and costly that it is seldom realized. In "Being and Seeming" on March 15, Emerson called for society to seek its needed cure in "a wise exploring of the power of man. We want faith in Human Nature. . . ."[49] And in the concluding Cambridge lecture, read in late March and entitled "Holiness," Emerson declared that one who desires holiness must learn nature's revelation that the highest dwells within. It was because Jesus knew this that he, more than any other man in history, seemed to have "a just estimate of man's worth."[50] These views later found their way into Judd's creative works, particularly into his first novel.

Judd may well have heard Emerson deliver "The Divinity School Address" to the senior class in the Divinity School on Sunday evening, July 15, 1838, before he left Cambridge for Northampton. Even when Judd returned to Cambridge in September, the effects of Emerson's words were still reverberating. Yet we have no record of Judd's reacting one way or the other to the storm that erupted in the Unitarian washbowl, to borrow a phrase from Emerson. But for Judd, Emerson had undoubtedly gone too far this time in his frontal attack on institutionalized religion. After all, Judd loved the church and the Christ of the church, and he must have shuddered at Emerson's blasphemy in taking away from Christ his unique divinity. Judd, as he indicated in *Philo*, found the Transcendentalists hollow, principally because Christ was not accorded his rightful place in their view.

VIII   *At Harvard Divinity School: Jones Very*

As has already been mentioned, Judd had, while at Harvard, a deepseated need for a close human friendship. In fact, his pervasive need for human sympathy, for a rare and costly friendship with another human being of lofty mind, for a Damon to his Pythias, might be called Judd's Harvard crisis. "It is a notion," he wrote, "which I humor myself in indulging, that there is, somewhere in the world, somebody *just like me*, whose modes of thought, habits of philosophizing, intellectual and religious training and discipline, whose aspirations, hopes, doubts, whose idiosyncrasies and eccentricities are the counterpart of my own."[51]

It is interesting to speculate that Judd might have seen—or thought he saw—in Jones Very, his divinity school classmate and Harvard tutor in freshman Greek, what he was looking for. On a manuscript copy of a Jones Very poem—"The New Birth"[52]— dated September 1838 and now among the Judd Papers at Harvard, Judd wrote, "By My Friend, Jones Very."[53] Was Very the friend, the congenial heart, Judd longed for communion with? The evidence points in that direction.

In September 1836, a few days after it was published and a year before entering the Divinity School, Very read Emerson's *Nature;* and the markings and marginalia of his copy indicate how much he subscribed—even literally—to Emerson's paean on the likeness of man and nature. On April 4, 1838, the divinity student, armed with his lecture on "Epic Poetry," journeyed out to Concord to meet Emerson.[54] Emerson was taken with this one who sought a mystical identification with Christ, and he introduced him at a later meeting of the Transcendental Club. Shortly after the beginning of the 1838–39 academic term, Very began to preach his own version of Christian idealism to the Harvard freshmen. Word soon spread through the school that Mr. Tutor Very was insane. He announced on September 13 that his mystical identification with Christ was complete; the next day he shocked his freshmen students with the declaration that he was now infallible; and on the following day, September 15, he was carted off to his home in Salem.

On the same day that his friend left Cambridge, Judd wrote a letter, mystical in tone, and quite out of keeping with his usual style. Arethusa Hall indicates only that the letter was addressed to "To ———." She normally noted, if only by initials, to whom Judd's letters were addressed. The best guess is that Judd's mystically cryptic letter of September 15 followed his friend Very to Salem. "If the muse has departed," Judd wrote, "does not her haunt still remain? . . . The bay is still there, with its many islands, like the repose of thought, amidst the eddyings of everlasting being. . . . An oppressiveness has settled on my spirits, for a dissipation of which, I hasted to seek the influences

of my friend, confidante, nurse, Nature. . . ." Judd concluded
the letter: "I love sometimes to utter myself; and the communion
of congenial hearts,—that rare waterspring in this desert
world,—is dearer to me than all things else this side of eternity.
God bless you, as my Lamb says. So prays sincerely your
friend."[55]

If the letter of September 15 was a letter to Very, then Judd's
letter of November 5, addressed "To the Same," would also have
been to Very. On October 17, Very was released, after a short
stay, from Charlestown's McLean Hospital for the Insane. In the
letter, Judd made mention of his "irrepressible longing for
sympathy" and to the fact that some persons possess one point of
excellence, some another. It is, however, when "we meet
someone with whom we sympathize on all points" that "our souls
rush together, like sister-angels!" The elements of the perfect
character are intelligence, sentiment, and virtue. "These
qualities, blended, relieved, sustained, matured, constitute a
character which we gaze upon with loving admiration. . . . The
actual of the ideal we sometimes see in the world."[56]

In the winter of 1838 and the spring of 1839, Very went about
contacting his friends, warning them of the immediate danger of
forfeiting all possibility of reconciliation with God. He had
concluded that what was required for personal deliverance was
the deliberate surrender of whatever meant the most to a
person. Only through such an extreme, even agonizing sacrificial
act could the dominant in one's character be destroyed, sin be
suppressed, and purgation be accomplished. He had exorcised
from his own bosom his love of beauty.[57] Elizabeth Peabody was
told by Very that she would have to sacrifice her love of truth;
Dr. William Ellery Channing, his love of rectitude; and Bronson
Alcott, his spiritual curiosity. In late March 1839, Very, it seems,
carried his saving mission to Cambridge. Another letter to "To
——" indicates that Judd and a friend spent April 1 in a stroll
through Mount Auburn, the beautiful Cambridge cemetery that
was a favorite haunt of both Very and Judd. Apparently Very
attempted to inform Judd—and the evidence does point to Very
as the friend—that the dominant in his character that should be
destroyed was too much spiritual assurance; that was the sin he
should suppress; but Judd failed fully to understand at the time.
"We were speaking," Judd wrote on April 2, a day later, "of a
sense of unworthiness before God. Did you allude to the subject

because you thought I cherished too much assurance?"[58] Judd
then defended his assurance which alone, for him, gave life
meaning.

Some coolness—some misunderstanding even—may have
developed between the friends, as other letters to "To ———"
show. Perhaps Judd found it difficult to accept his friend's
increasingly Messianic pose. Nevertheless, he made at least one
final attempt to salvage a friendship that had particular
significance for him. In a meeting with Very early in Judd's third
year in divinity school, Judd pled with Very to renew and
continue their friendship. But Judd's only effort to establish a
lasting friendship with a Transcendentalist failed. In a note
headed "Bro. Very. Sept 22, 1839,"[59] Judd carefully recorded
what might well have been his last conversation with Very, who
was now advocating "unconsciousness" as a mystical way of
meeting or avoiding life. "When you are wholly unconscious,
then shall you rise and go to any man's house," Very said, "and he
will make you welcome." Very got up to leave, but, addressing
Judd, said: "You think you see me, but you do not. You can only
see me by finding me in yourself. And if you find me in yourself,
you will not wish to see me." As a parting plea, Judd asked if they
might at least correspond with one another. "A letter may be
written," Very replied, "but I shall be wholly unconscious of it. If
I find a piece of paper and your name is written on it, I shall not
know it. — I cannot tarry about these things." And he left.

Nevertheless, after Very's Emerson-edited *Essays and Poems*
was published by Little, Brown in September 1839, Judd, as a
coda to the recently concluded friendship, wrote a sympathetic
review of the little book—a review that anticipated Judd's own
subsequent reactions to adverse criticisms of his published
literary efforts. The review was not published until Miss Hall
included it in her biography. In fact, there is no evidence that
Judd had been commissioned by any journal to write the review.
But he did know the book; he did know the poet; he knew the
nature of the work and how it could and should be appreciated.

To understand Very's poetry, Judd insisted, one must realize
that the poetry was not a product of the poet's intellect. It had its
origin in, it was the product of, the soul; and a "a genuine product
of the soul, whether it be great or small, deserves a reverential
consideration. It should be examined by its own standards."[60]
Likewise, to judge poetry, one must judge the poet; the poet and

the work must be viewed as one. Even the "design is alone appreciable through, and it can alone be understood by knowing what he is."[61] And further, Judd asked, "Why should a man who speaks from personal, boundless, authoritative depths of his own nature trim and palaver to the public taste? What is public taste to him? *If there be souls like his own, they will appreciate what he says.* If not, how vain the task of accommodation to shallow and partial intellects! No power of criticism can make a piece of clay lustrous as a flower: the flower, though it be the humblest, shows its own colors, exhales its own fragrance."[62]

IX   A Young Man's Account of His Conversion from Calvinism (1838)

Judd too broke into print during his Cambridge days. As a second-year divinity student, he came at last to feel that he could now, in a dispassionate way, give the New England Unitarians an account of his conversion from Calvinism. In a series of letters addressed to W——n and published in the *Christian Register* in early 1838, he detailed what he considered the difficulties presented the thinker by Calvinism, reviewed his conversion, and proceeded again, as he had earlier in "Cardiagraphy," to defend Unitarianism, maintaining that Christ had come on earth not to create a new race of beings, but to elevate the existing race to its original purity. He also saw the possibility of a Utopia on earth since the doctrines proclaimed by the Unitarians should "subvert and utterly demolish, through the world, every system of oppression and degradation, religious, moral, and political,"[63] a contention that is basic to an understanding of the Mons Christi portion of *Margaret*. The American Unitarian Association was delighted by the series of letters, so much so that it hurriedly brought out in March 1838 a thirty-four-page reprinting of them under the title *A Young Man's Account of His Conversion from Calvinism. A Statement of Facts.*

X   *Divinity School Graduate*

Despite expected coolness from members of his family, despite health problems in 1838 that forced him to leave the Divinity School for a short period, despite a lack of financial support from his father and the debt he inevitably incurred, and despite his apparently disappointing search for a deep and abiding friendship with a kindred spirit, Judd graduated from the Divinity School in July 1840. He noted in his journal:

Cambridge, July 17, 1840.—My studies are over, my profession acquired, my work before me. My bodily health at least good, my energy vigorous. My heart, O my heart! is it sanctified yet? Am I humble? Life—*and* am I prepared for it, and *its?* Heaven—am I thither tending, and thither taking men's souls? Nine years ago, the first of June, found me commencing my studies at Hadley Academy. Three years—how quickly passed! The choicest, best part of my life, how gone! What have they carried me through? No matter now. I am a better and a calmer man. I have few agitations, know few griefs. Could name one or two things, but they are trifles. I enter the theatre of the world to act my part. What shall I accomplish? With what object link myself, to what idea give an impulse? Christ, I am thine, wholly thine. Sanctify me to thyself; make me wise for thy sake; make me energetic for thy sake; make me influential for thy sake.[64]

CHAPTER 2

The Liberal Minister at Augusta

I Settled In

A week and a half before his graduation from the Divinity School, Judd agreed to supply the pulpit of the Unitarian Church in Augusta, Maine, for six weeks. On Sunday morning, July 26, 1840, he preached his first sermon; and immediately his parishioners—people he found both intelligent and serious—began to urge him to consider a permanent appointment; yet, as he noted in his journal, he felt "unhomed here."[1] But pressures mounted from the parish committee, and on August 26 Judd agreed to remain for a year. But, because of an earlier commitment, Judd left Augusta a week later for a four-week's preaching engagement in Deerfield, Massachusetts. While away, he spent some time in Westhampton, visiting scenes of his boyhood—his grandfather's old mansion, the house he lived in as a boy, the old store, and the orchard where the black walnuts planted by his father were now grown to large trees.

By late September, he was again at his ministerial duties in Augusta. On Thursday, October 1, all of Maine's Unitarian clergymen gathered there. The Reverend Frederic Henry Hedge—whose trips from Bangor down to Boston were always sufficient reason for a convening of the Transcendental Club or the Hedge Club, as it came to be called—preached the ordination sermon. The following Sunday, Judd preached from the text, "Woe is unto me, if I preach not the gospel"; and he threw himself with abandon into the multifarious chores his ministerial office demanded.

Yet he was lonely for the companionship of old friends. On its way to the sea, the Kennebec River, which flowed past his quarters, only served to remind him, perhaps, of how far removed he was from his family in the Valley of the Connecticut. Early, though, in 1841, Judd developed a romantic interest in Jane Elizabeth Williams, the daughter of United States Senator Reuel Williams, one of the founders of the East Parish Church. On August 9, the banns were cried; and on August 31, the couple were married. The next morning, they set off on their honeymoon for Northampton to meet the groom's family. For nearly a month, the newlyweds revisited the haunts of Judd's childhood, "—the old familiar scenes, the spots, in some instances, where the dark waters of sorrow had overwhelmed his soul."[2]

Married now and no longer regarding Augusta as a temporary way station, Judd threw himself with renewed vigor into his work—to preaching, to championing several of the reform movements of the day, to lecturing on the lyceum circuit, to playing a leadership role among the Unitarians of Maine, and to writing his creative works. He caused the name of the church to be changed from East Parish to Christ Church to reflect the emphasis of his ministry and the true nature of the church. Never one to fear innovations, he wanted to preach also among the pines on Malta Hill, a high spot overlooking the Kennebec; and with his own hands he prepared the place. He delighted in accompanying the children on nature walks and in meeting with the young ladies for literary discussion. On October 5, 1851, eleven years after his ordination, Judd preached a sermon in which he reviewed the accomplishments of his pastorate. "The first year of my ministry," he told his congregation, ". . . was a pretty fair index to what the whole has been. God had thoroughly indoctrinated me in the great truths of Christ and the church, peace, temperance, recreation, human nature, human duty, human destiny, before my settlement; and I have only had occasion to mature, improve upon, and apply those views since."[3] Ever, he assured them, his purpose had been to preach Christ. This, he also might have added, was the motivating force not only back of his sermons, but also the motivating force back of his lectures, his efforts on behalf of reform, and his creative works.

II   *The Preacher*

A. *"Suffer Little Children to Come unto Me"*

Judd's first two published sermons indicated something of his particular concern for children. The first—entitled "The Little Coat"—was published—perhaps in late 1840—by the Unitarian Sunday-School Society and later by the American Reform Tract and Book Society. The sermon, addressed especially to mothers, urged them to see that their children were provided coats for their minds and souls, coats made up of holy words and deeds of mothers. "It is yours," Judd said, "to dress a new, living spirit; to cut out and make for it celestial attire; it is yours to give it the robe of immortality."[4]

Judd preached "The Beautiful Zion" at Christ Church on July 4, 1841. In the sermon, in a plain and simple manner, he set forth his view as to what the aims of the Christian church should be and what he, as pastor, should do to enable the church to realize those aims. So important did he consider the sermon that he printed it at his own expense and distributed it to each family in his congregation. Among other things, Judd declared that "the beauty of Zion will be enhanced by the number of those that come to her altars."[5] Children were among those who should come; they should not be denied church membership. "I know," he said, "of but one pre-requisite for church-membership; that is, love to Christ."[6]

B.   A Moral Review of the Revolutionary War

Judd decided that, beginning in January 1842, he would deliver once a month a Sunday-evening discourse on some moral topic he considered to be of general importance. Meanwhile, the young minister was rapidly acquiring a place of enviable importance in the community; and on January 8, he was appointed Chaplain of both houses of the Maine Legislature. His January discourse on "Washingtonianism"—a popular temperance movement—was delivered to a packed church and met with popular favor. Consequently, he was assured of a host of eager auditors when he presented in February his views on "Popular Amusements in Connection with Morals and Religion." However, on Monday, March 14, the day after his discourse on the evils of the Revolutionary War, both houses of the legislature unceremoniously revoked his appointment as chaplain. His own congregation, nevertheless, stood with him; after all, he had not spoken as a politician, but as a minister who, deep down, was convinced that even the most righteous wars were wrong.

But in his defense, he felt that he must publish what he had said so that all fair men might calmly and deliberately judge the true spirit of his remarks. The forty-eight-page publication bore the title *A Moral Review of the Revolutionary War, Or Some of the Evils of That Event Considered. A Discourse Delivered at the Unitarian Church, Sabbath Evening, March 13th, 1842. With An Introductory Address, And Notes.* The introductory address was directed *"To all who love the Lord Jesus Christ, and would be obedient to His Heavenly Mission."* [7] Judd, in his five-page introduction, attempted to clarify his own long-held position from the standpoint of his being a minister, a man, and an American citizen. War was, he was convinced, "wrong in principle, erroneous in policy, corrupt in practice, [and] disastrous in effect," for in any war "the best men are unnaturalized and depraved, and the best of purposes sullied and deformed." Nothing, he was certain, was ever gained by war that could not, with a thousand-fold advantage, have been gained by peace. He singled out the Revolutionary War—the holiest war on record—in order to drive his point home that no good ever came even from the most justifiable of wars. His purpose had not been to reflect unfavorably upon "the Fathers of the Revolution, as noble a race of men as the earth affords *in every other capacity.*" [8] Yet separation from Great Britain, Judd contended, was inevitable and would have come about, in time, in a bloodless manner because man's desire to be free would have been realized in the natural evolutionary political processes.

In his Sunday-evening remarks on March 13, Judd reviewed the history of the colonists' struggle with Great Britain and concluded that it was not a popular war but one the people, if they had had their way, would have rejected. As proof, Judd pointed to the wholesale desertion of American troops after the first major defeat. The inevitable results of the war were social corruption, despotism, denial of minority rights, encouragement to lawlessness and plundering, and, in general, the excuse for inhumane acts of appalling barbarity. Judd ended his discourse: "I close with a single reflection. If our Revolutionary War, which has been deemed the holiest war on record, *and which I freely grant to have been the holiest war on record,* was corrupt enough to sink it to the condemnation of every good man's judgment and conscience, *what shall we say of war in general*?" Judd then noted, "The last sentence contains the pith, spirit, aim, and object of the whole discourse."[9]

But Judd was not through yet. In the notes appended to *A Moral Review,* he listed twenty-eight reasons why war could never be justified, ranging from his contention that "Christ has in effect wholly forbidden war" to war "exhumes the Indian tomahawk" and "sends souls to the bar of the Lord without penitence or atonement."[10]

The publication of *A Moral Review* only served to broaden the controversy. Judd, however, was inundated with letters of congratulation and sympathy. On April 29, 1842, the American Peace Society, meeting in Boston, passed a "resolve of sympathy with the Rev. Mr. Judd, in the persecution he has suffered, of admiration for his courage, and of approval of the great object of the sermon as correct and Christian."[11] The Reverend Samuel Joseph May—fellow Unitarian minister and, at the time, General Agent of the Massachusetts Anti-Slavery Society—wrote to Judd from South Scituate on May 10: "Your discourse, my brother, has already brought down condemnation upon you—and you will have to bear yet more."[12]

The reaction of the press, on the other hand, was mixed but generally sympathetic toward the minister. Most of the newspapers took the position that what Judd said in his pulpit to his own congregation should not have raised the hackles of the legislators. In fact, the Belfast, Maine, *Republican Journal* on May 6 went so far as to declare the whole matter a silly one and the sermon that provoked it to be not so full of "horribles" as full of "mere bugbears."

Yet the legislature continued to nurse its patriotic wrath; and when it assembled a year later, there were enough of its members still so incensed by the intolerable remarks of its erstwhile chaplain that they did not wish to hear prayers from such a source. If, indeed, the sentiments expressed the year before *did* come from the minister's heart, then they came from a heart desperately wicked; and the Scripture teaches that the prayers of the wicked are an abomination in the sight of the Lord. Such views prevailed during the 1843 session, and Judd was not reappointed until January 8, 1844.

C. *The Busy Minister*

Meanwhile, the temporarily excommunicated chaplain gave himself without reserve to the many ministerial and literary tasks he had set for himself. In the spring of 1842, he attempted unsuccessfully to bring the various churches in Augusta together in a union meeting of all denominations. "This proposal," he explained to the Augusta ministers, "only contemplates a single meeting, for a single evening; a one hour's union and conciliation of the scattered members of the Christian body about their common Head and Master, Christ; . . . a momentary realization, here on earth, of that heaven we hope so soon to enter, and whose level we must so soon be compelled to take."[13] But he was denied this momentary heavenly realization.

Rebuffed, Judd turned his eyes increasingly toward his own congregation and to the novel he had been planning for a year or more. He continued to meet with the young ladies for "literary improvement"; he encouraged social gatherings in private homes for the general improvement of his flock. In the summer of 1843 he journeyed down to Westhampton and Norwich, seeking more "hints for the romance he had on hand."[14] And by the time he was reinstated by the legislature, he was well into Part II of *Margaret*. Judd spent a good part of May 1844 in New York City, returning to Augusta by the scenic route up the Hudson and through the Berkshire highlands. In June, he lectured to the Sabbath-school children on ornithology and, in early fall, planned a rural festival for his parishioners on Malta Hill, where he preached his sermon on "The Church in the Woods." In late fall, his first daughter was born; and about November 22, he completed *Margaret*.

D. *". . . For the Better Preparation of Spiritual Food"*

All the while, the studious minister was amassing a larger and larger library; and, more and more, he came to feel a compelling need for a more spacious study. His well-to-do father-in-law—lawyer, banker, land speculator, dam builder, industrialist, and politician—gave him a lot next to his own home and advanced Judd the funds to build a house of his own design. On November 21, 1846, at the consecration of the new house, Judd gathered his congregation in his study, the largest room in the Gothic-style

house, and declared that this room "was for the better
preparation of spiritual food for them."[15]

Arethusa Hall, who came in 1846 for a two-year stay in
Augusta and who probably lived, while there, with her nephew
and his family in the new house, has left us a record in her
memoirs of some of the titles Judd had accumulated in his
spiritual kitchen. The books reveal perhaps better than any
other direct evidence we have the scope and breadth of Judd's
liberal—even Transcendental—reading at the time, the scope
and breadth of which he or Arethusa seemed careful to hide in
the correspondence of his that has been preserved. However, it
was through Judd, Miss Hall said, that she "began to have access
to books of a different character from any I had read, such as
Channing's and Emerson's."[16] Together, she said, they read
Carlyle. "Carlyle," according to Miss Hall, "introduced me to
Goethe, Schiller, Lessing, Richter, and other German writers,
whose line of thought was widely different from what I had been
accustomed to in books which I had read; and it was very
attractive to me."[17]

There were novels, books of poetry, history, and travel, and
biographies in Judd's library. Miss Hall wrote:

Sylvester Judd's library contained many books leading into new lines of
thought. "Wilhelm Meister" and Goethe's "Correspondences with a
Child," also some specimens of the writing of Richter and Fichte,
opened vistas into new fields of thought. The lives of Goethe, Mozart,
Beethoven, etc., were full of interest. George Sand I began to know in
her "Consuélo." Bayley's [sic] "Festus" commanded attention. Hedge's
"Prose Writers of Germany" was liberalizing. Plato's "Divine
Dialogues," with the "Apology of Socrates," were charming. The
"Vestiges of Creation," and, I will add, some portions of Davis's "Divine
Revelations," were an opening wedge to "infidelity." . . . The
"Christian Examiner" was enlightening, and Parker's "Sermons,"
commended themselves to my reason. All these influences, added to
the effect of Sylvester's preaching, which I constantly heard when I
was in Augusta, and the light I obtained from conversation with him,
made me quite ready to pass over into the Unitarian ranks at the close
of 1848.[18]

E. *The Convert as Transcendentalist*

Judd had won perhaps his only convert from the families of his
father or his mother or from among his own brothers and sisters,

for that matter. Miss Hall became, in time, an avowed Transcendentalist, as the published excerpts from her private notebooks and journals show. Like Emerson, she came to feel "the currents of Universal Being" flowing through her; and her heart, she wrote in 1879, "seems to beat in unison with the great heart of Nature. It is good to be leisurely alone with the Soul of the Universe, to feel at one with the informing Spirit of the Whole, unfathomable, incomprehensible though it be."[19] She found God revealed in Nature and tried to square her life, physically and morally, with the laws inherent in the Universe. Thus, she experienced in her spirit "the emotion of *religion* in its deepest, most reverential sense,—a sense too deep for words, but one of yearning for union with the Infinite Ideal, and for the utmost possible attainment of the Infinite Perfection."[20] Jesus, however, she held not to be exceptional in *kind* from other men, although "in character, he may well be placed among the highest Sons of God that have been produced in the human race."[21]

Had Judd lived past his fortieth year, he might well have been taken aback at the religious "infidelity" of his converted aunt. He might have approved of her mystical bent, her worship of the God she found in Nature, and her longing for perfection; but Judd would never have joined her in the Emersonian view that Jesus was *a* son of God, rather than *the* unique Son of God. It was on this point that Judd most definitely parted company with the Transcendentalists. It was because of their inadequate Christology, or lack of it, that Judd in *Philo* declared them to be spiritually empty, having fed too often on their own inner beings. In fact, Judd preached more frequently on the mission and nature of Christ than on any other theme: "The Indwelling Christ," "Christ the Light of the World," "Christ the Hope of the World," "Christ the Resurrection and the Life," "Christ Our Righteousness," "The Cross of Christ," and "Christ a Mediator," to cite but a few sermon titles.

F.   *The Minister as Unitarian*

And Judd never tired of proclaiming the glories of Christ along with the glories of Unitarianism. In fact, to him, the truth of Unitarianism was the unqualified truth as it was in Christ; to Judd, Unitarianism was the Gospel—virginal, verdant, beautiful, and God-given. Unitarianism, Judd preached, brought "Christ back from an unnatural and factitious place in the universe,"[22]

and now in Christ everyone could become a brother of man and a
child of God. Unitarianism, Judd repeatedly told his congregation, was a system of absolute truth that was essential,
continuous, and contemporaneous with rational being, yet,
contrary to a charge of the Transcendentalists, it *did* touch the
feelings. It affirmed the unity of the revelation of God in
Scripture and in nature, gathering all things—the atonement, the
communion of saints, the one body, the one church—into one.
The doctrines of Unitarianism were whatever Christ taught and
"whatever truth God from creation has been pouring, from the
bright urn of central reality, over the realms of nature, or into
the recesses of the soul."[23] Unitarianism declared the unity of
God, sole and indivisible. Christ, however, was not God but was
"included in the circumference of the Unity of God."[24] "I
believe," Judd preached, "that Christ came on this atoning,
unifying, unitarianizing errand, to reconcile or make us all at one
with God."[25] "We in Christ are in God,"[26] Judd affirmed. In July
1849, in a sermon entitled "The Communion for Sinners," Judd
declared that Christ lived, labored, and died for the cleansing of
the human race, that his blood stands for his life, and that his life
was shed for the remission of sins.

G. *"The True Dignity of Politics"*

On May 26, 1850, Judd preached a sermon on the topic of "The
True Dignity of Politics." Here was a sermon the legislators
assembled in Augusta could vigorously applaud, and the next
morning an elated House of Representatives ordered "that a
committee be raised to wait on Rev. Mr. Judd and request, for
publication, a copy of his sermon delivered last evening, at Christ
Church, on the 'True Dignity of Politics.' "[27] Judd equated the
politician with the statesman and declared politics to be a "grave
and venerable vocation."[28] This, no doubt, was music to the ears
of the politicians who heard his sermon. Reminiscent of Thoreau
in "Civil Disobedience," Judd lamented, though, that often there
was too much government, too great an exercise of governmental
power, and too much interference in private matters. But what
were the alternatives? They were no government that would
result in something akin to anarchy or a wise government that
would suggest as well as decree and that would encourage the
good as well as repress the vicious. The basis of any government,

in Judd's view, was the will of God as revealed in Scripture, nature, reason, and conscience. The true politician likes to feel, Judd said, that he is guided by an instinctive consciousness of rectitude. Well and good. But he should be reminded also that "that instinctive consciousness of rectitude is merely an offshoot or upbubbling from the eternal rectitude, whose influence circumscribes and underflows us all."[29]

The absolute and the divine were the standards by which all human action was to be governed, and politics would become more and more perfect the closer it approximated the divine idea that men should govern as God would have them govern. Asserting that America in 1850 was the culmination of God's dealing with nations for the past six thousand years, Judd asked, "Eddying through the dimness of time, on what shore shall the hope of Humanity culminate and resurge in everlasting beauty, if not ours?"[30] On May 30, 1850, the printer for the state was ordered to publish a thousand copies of the sermon for the use of the house.

H.   *The Preacher as Writer*

On July 27, 1852, Judd wrote his Worcester friend, the Reverend Edward Everett Hale, a letter indicating the importance Judd assigned his three published creative works in the total context of his ministry.

For years I have been burying myself, plans, hopes, speculations, in something I call the church, the true, Christian church. In "Margaret" the thing is broadly hinted at; in "Philo" it comes up in another shape; in "Richard Edney" it becomes an assumed fact. It is, of course, "catholic"; it is, of course, "orthodox"; it is *the* church; it is "holy and apostolical"; and it is, to the core, Unitarian. To these ideas I am gradually bringing my own parish.

There is no salvation for this world but in Unitarianism,—the one God, the one humanity, the one communion of all souls, the unity in God of science, art, religion, life, earth and heaven, time and eternity.[31]

Judd wanted his fellow ministers to join him, not in writing novels and dramatic poems, but in publishing to the world Unitarian principles, views, and plans. On November 2, 1852, in a letter to the Reverend Mr. Palfrey of Belfast, Maine, Judd proposed a volume to answer to the spirit of inquiry abroad in the land. He wrote:

I am willing to take all the risk of publication; and what I want is, that any of us whose minds have been exercised in this matter should give to the world a discourse upon it. You take up one point, I another, &c., &c. I want we should show a kind of organic, unitary front. I am tired of so much personality. For my own part, I have several discourses I might put in. Have you not preached some sermons that are *just the thing*? I repeat, I take *all the risk*.[32]

I. The Church in a Series of Discourses *(1854)*

The volume Judd proposed was published in 1854, the year after Judd's death. But rather than sermons by several hands, the volume, it seems, is only a collection of Judd's sermons, thus perpetuating the cult of personality Judd deplored. The book, entitled *The Church in a Series of Discourses*, was a 274-page book and contained fourteen sermons on Christian baptism, Gospel conversion, the nature of the church, the communion, children as communicants, and so on. Running through the sermons, however, as a recurring motif is the view that the church has a special responsibility for children, who have a "birth-relation" to the church. The argument is that just as children by birth are made citizens of the state, just so by birth are they born into the church, which is more universal than any existing state. In a sermon entitled "The Church Hereditable," Judd asserted that "no church-covenant is complete that does not include the children; that it is not only not complete, but radically and fatally defective."[33] The regeneration of the children was to occur in the church, not out of it. Sermon VIII is entitled "We Send Children to Heaven, But Dare Not Admit Them to the Church." Sermon IX is entitled "Children to Be Communicants." And in his sermon on "Christian Baptism," Judd admitted that Christian baptism seemed most appropriate for repentant sinners of mature years. But then what about the children? "I answer," Judd said, "baptism is not, indeed, a sign of the purification of children . . . who have never sinned; it is a sign of the purity *into what it is hoped children may grow. . . . It is the seal of the covenant which the Church makes with its children."* [34] Judd was sure that the gravest concern of the church should be for the welfare of its children around whom the salutary forces of religion should be thrown.

Thus, when Judd committed himself to deliver on January 6 in Boston the first Thursday Lecture of 1853, he decided upon what to him was the compelling theme—"The Birthright Church." Late December 1852 and the early days of the new year found him gathering and condensing his views, expressed in many sermons, into one discourse, views which he was eager to lay before a largely clerical audience. He finished the manuscript on Monday following the delivery of his New Year's sermon and prepared to leave for Boston on Tuesday, January 4. But he fell sick while he waited for the cars and was not able to leave Augusta. He died on January 26.

J. The Birthright Church

The sermon— *The Birthright Church: A Discourse . . . Designed For "Thursday Lecture" In Boston, Jan. 6, 1853*—was published posthumously in the early spring by the Boston publisher Crosby and Nichols and reprinted in Augusta in 1854 for the Maine Association of the Unitarian Church. Earlier Judd had presented his views before the Maine Association, an organization Judd worked hard to perfect, before the 1852 Autumnal Convention of Unitarians in Baltimore, and eagerly he anticipated doing the same before the Boston Unitarians. He planned to reiterate his fundamental position that the church, equally with the family and state, was of divine appointment and that in each a person found himself in an undeniable birth-relationship. Children were born into the church as surely as they were born into the family and into the state.

Judd wanted all people—children and adults—to feel that *all* of the church with *all* of its ordinances belonged to them. Children should grow up in the nurture and admonition of the church. No one ever thought differently, Judd had planned to proclaim, until the doctrine of total depravity raised its ugly head and declared that children are born corrupt, of the devil, and out of the Christian pale. The time had at last come, Judd felt, to correct this sad situation and to restore children to their birthright, to restore the birthright to all who had been deprived of it. Judd noted in his manuscript:

If there be a school of highest Christian discipline, a circle of highest Christian culture, a theatre of highest Christian action, a place of highest Christian life, peace, enjoyment, I contend that not only the children, but the great mass of the community, should be included in it.

And such a school, circle, theatre, place, is the church. I would take this which we call the church, with all its awfulness and beauty, all its beatitudes and obligations, and not wait to see if I can get here and there a man into it, but take it and carry it right under the whole bulk of the rising generation, and endeavor that they should be in it. I would carry it under the yet unborn generations, and see to it that all share in it as their birthright.[35]

What Judd really envisioned was a Christian social order, with the church radiating from the center to the circumference—a Christian social order much like that of Mons Christi in his novel *Margaret*. The result would be, once all people were in what Judd called the church-estate, that spirituality and Christian virtue would usher in an age of Millennial glory, which the church-system of 1853 could never bring about.

III   *The Reformer*

Judd was a preacher. Judd was a reformer. But sometimes it is difficult to know where Judd the minister ends and Judd the reformer begins. Yet Judd seems to have made a distinction between the two. "The moral reformer," he said, "must combine beauty in his manner, motives, and deeds, or he cannot persuade men. The moment one, in his spirit or expression, becomes ugly, though he be engaged in the best work in the world, he will enlist no sympathy, kindle no love, and, of course, accomplish nothing."[36] He, in the spirit of love, looked to enlightening, convincing, and persuading to bring about reform where reform was needed. According to Miss Hall, Judd said:

Our politicians and reformers, our conservatists and radicals, our woman's-rights men and man's-rights women, our orthodox and our heterodox, rum men and anti-rum men, slaveholders and abolitionists, have got to come to this,—the recognition of the reasonable soul; the observance of the sovereignty of ideas; the creed and covenant of our higher nature; . . . or, however we may have truth and right on our side, we shall find we are perpetually degenerating to the plane of bestiality and barbarism, and that the disintegration of those moral bonds that should forever unite us is rapidly hastening.[37]

Like Emerson and Thoreau, he wished to cast the weight of the reasonable individual on the side of right.

A. *Slavery*

His even-handed reasonableness was demonstrated in his stand on slavery. To be sure, Judd sensed deeply the wrongs of slavery—"that gigantic subject of gigantic difficulties."[38] Yet he would not allow slavery to become for him the all-absorbing evil. In fact, he did not advocate harsh treatment of the slaveholder, nor did he harshly denounce him. Perhaps he could be loved into repentence and reformation, Judd hoped.

This did not mean that Judd regarded slavery lightly. As he said at an Independence Day celebration on July 4, 1852, at Portland, "The positive and leading idea of our country, as distinguished from most others, is supposed to be liberty, the basis of which is reason and intelligence, virtue and religion,— liberty for all in all things. . . . I love this idea, and for this idea I love my country."[39] But slavery was *not* an idea of his country. Though legal, it could not possibly logically exist in a land of liberty. And his fervent hope was to see the foul and illogical blot of slavery removed. That men have inalienable rights—the slave included—was a fact that originated with God and was based on the harmony of certain basic ideas of heavenly origin. Perchance it was Judd's aversion to setting man against man or, worse, his horror at the prospects of armed conflict and the premonition of impending bloodshed that tempered his efforts on behalf of the slave.

B. *"Indian-driving"*

Judd was not so mild in his condemnation of those responsible for the treatment and plight of the Indian. "I think," he said at Portland, "we have dealt worse by the Indian than by the African. We exterminate the former; we domesticate the latter. We find the black man a peck of corn a week; we curse the red man with whiskey. I am sometimes astonished, that, in the varied philanthropies of the age, no advocate of the aboriginal population arises; that, where there is so much fervid denunciation of the wrongs of slaveholding, there are none to execrate that greater villany, Indian-driving."[40] A most flagrant case of injustice, American style, had been done them. The notion that their destiny to perish was decreed by America's destiny to span the continent was, to Judd, an utterly ridiculous argument from expediency. "Away with this doctrine of manifest destiny, which, on our lips and in this connection, means nothing more than consummate selfishness!"[41] he shouted to his July 4 audience.

C. *Intemperance*

Intemperance, to Judd, was a manifest evil, a large branch of the tree of evil, whose other branches — avarice, oppression of all sorts, hurtful ambition, and general injustice — were of the same stock. From its inception in 1840, Judd was interested in the work of the Washington Temperance Society and the movement it promoted, commonly known as Washingtonianism. The idea was that a reformed drunkard — one who had signed the pledge — would bring a wayward brother to a meeting where the reformed one would testify to the joys of his newfound life. Perhaps the idea of throwing the arm of support around the rum-drinker had its initial appeal for Judd. Even the pledge — "Come and sign the pledge as I did, and you'll be a happy man. Keep the pledge and all will come right again!" — Judd may have approved of. But what Judd perhaps frowned on was an insistence by William K. Mitchell, one of the Society's founders, that religion was not needed to bolster the convert's courage. In fact, he banned prayer in the meetings.

Judd, however, was sure that "moral suasion" alone was not sufficient. But the movement was important to the welfare of the people, and Judd sought to save it. Thus on February 2, 1845, he preached — and later published — a sermon entitled *A Discourse Touching the Causes and Remedies of Intemperance*. The trouble with Washingtonianism was that it was fostered by impulse and rested on sentiment rather than being grounded in a sound faith in the regenerative power of Christian love, Judd said. God was being left out.

What about laws to solve the problem? With obvious reference to the debate going on at the time over the proposed Maine Law — the first statewide statute in America that would be designed to outlaw the sale of alcoholic beverages except for medicinal purposes — Judd declared that such a law would have a tendency to nourish the evil it deplored, would not address the affections of those whose business it touched, would win no love, and would convert no man's will. It would provide, he said, "the incentives to public corruption, in the form of perjury, false-witness, concealment, tergiversation, pretence, bribery, [and] barratry." It would lead to "the operation of a dread resilience" and "to that something worse, an exacerbated collision of public sentiment where force shall be repelled by force."[42] In short, to attempt to bring about reform by resorting to law was contrary to the true principles of moral reform as Judd conceived those principles. Nevertheless, the legislators of Maine, some of whom must have heard Judd's sermon, voted into law the next year a statewide prohibition on the sale of beverage alcohol for nonmedicinal purposes.

It is interesting—but not surprising—that Judd in his sermon should trace the roots of intemperance in New England back to the stern Puritan fathers, who made no provision for the recreational needs of the people upon whom the cares of life pressed so heavily. Thus they betook themselves for recreation to the cup since they had no dances, parlor games, musical entertainments, art exhibits, fairs, tea parties, or rural festivals. Even the very ministers who denounced sports drank rum, and the parents who whipped their children for playing Saturday nights drank rum. In fact, Judd said, "To take a glass of liquor was a cheap, summary, expeditious, unobtrusive way of self-recreation."[43] Or, as Judd reiterated later, "Rum became the recreative element to our ancestors."[44]

Thus, Judd argued, any prohibition that ignored the recreative needs of the drinker had little chance of any real success and would fail completely to bring about any lasting good if provisions were not made toward the spiritual regeneration of the drunkard, which, of course, in Judd's view no law was or could be designed to provide. But with man's need for recreation in mind, Judd advocated, as a first step in the right direction, the opening of attractive coffee houses, furnished with books and newspapers and other "pleasures, relaxations, and means of agreeable excitements,"[45] such as music and carefully regulated dancing. In every way, man's love of the beautiful in sight, sound, and motion needed to be encouraged. Christians, too, must exemplify the truth as it is in Jesus, and the church must make it possible for the tempted soul to find the strength that is in God and religion, else the rum bottle would continue to be the solace of New England, maugre pledges, societies, and laws.

D. *Treatment of Criminals*

Judd's interest in the reform movements of the day included a concern for a more reasonable treatment of criminals and the abolition of capital punishment. Prisons, Judd felt, should be primarily places of regeneration, not primarily places of punishment. No human being was so depraved as to be beyond

hope of reclamation. According to Miss Hall, Judd adopted in full
the spirit of the old proverb, "Beneath every jacket there lives a
man."[46] The very persistence of crime, Judd was sure, was largely
due to society's penchant for never wanting to forgive the guilty.
"I know it is a received maxim," Miss Hall quoted him as saying,
"that not the severity, but the certainty, of punishment prevents
crime. I have little confidence in either mode. We must seek to
reform the criminal. The most dangerous men, the dark prowlers
through our communities, are those whom we have punished in
our prisons."[47] And as for capital punishment, Judd felt it to be
totally contrary to the spirit of the New Testament, totally
inexpedient in preventing crime, and totally unthinkable as an
exercise of judicial power.

E.   *Nonresistance, War, Military Intervention . . .*

It is perhaps appropriate that what was likely Judd's last
lyceum appearance should have been devoted to delivering a
lecture on "nonresistance" before his Augusta townsmen in
December of 1852. Right off, he denied that war ever aided
civilization. He could point to whole civilizations buried by
violence, art destroyed beyond recovery, and the ancient
archives of Asia Minor and Egypt gone because of senseless
destruction. Judd deplored the recent war against Mexico and
the attempt of the United States to open up Japan through a
display of force. He deplored equally the doctrine of intervention as an example of mistaken means to accomplish what might
seem a justifiable end. "Well," he told his neighbors, "we want to
help Hungary. And what is the first thought that offers itself to
the popular instinct? Why, pour in between the invader and the
patriots a score of our gallant troops; shoot down the Austrian,
beat back the Russian. The spirit evoked is that of the ramrod."[48]
Such action overlooked the power of moral force and betrayed
the savageness of the United States foreign policy. "Intervention!" Judd exclaimed. "The most solid, enduring, effective
intervention America can give, is summarily that of her example.
A great and good republic, prosperous, stable, happy, and pure,
on these western shores, is the most formidable and terrible
thing to tyrants that can be conceived."[49] The strength of
America, Judd declared, was in her freedom of religion which
could be held up to the envy of the rest of the world. "These are
our weapons of warfare,"[50] he said. In the mission of Christ is

seen the mission of every Christian nation; Christ came to the world on a mission of love. He decried the doctrine of "An eye for an eye, a tooth for a tooth." The minister in Judd the reformer demanded that he assert, "I am supremely a Christian, being neither pagan nor Jew, unbeliever nor transcendentalist. I do not presume to vindicate Christ's doctrine; I dare not qualify it; I trust I have too much Christian honor to blink it. I accept it. As a Christian disciple, I would study it; as a Christian teacher, I would enforce it."[51]

IV   *The Lecturer*

At the time of his death, Judd had committed himself for a number of lyceum appearances as his schedule cards among the Judd Papers at Harvard show. According to Miss Hall, Judd's lectures on "The Beautiful," "Language," and "The Dramatic Element in the Bible" were among his most popular and most often repeated—lectures not called forth in response to the evils of the day, but lectures on topics of timeless and popular interest. Although Judd kept the reformer out of the lectures, he did not succeed in submerging the minister.

A. *"The Beautiful"*

Judd's "The Beautiful" bears a close resemblance to the section on "Beauty" in Emerson's *Nature*, especially in Judd's contention that, in the bright light of day, things take on a beauty, even a fairylike appearance. In the polar regions, light, "striking across the inequalities of glacier-land, portrays castles and caves."[52] Light enhances even the kraal of the Hottentot, the subterranean abode of the Greenlander, and the American Indian hails its glimmer in the greenwood. Christ came proclaiming that he was the light of the world. God wished him to be beautiful, pleasing, and attractive to the human mind in his person and in the beauty of his ideas.

If mankind is to embrace it, then even religion must be beautiful, Judd declared. If prayer were not beautiful, man could not take pleasure in it. Man recognizes the beauty in consistency of character and in a well-spent life. Like Emerson, Judd found the desire for beauty to be a deepseated need of the human mind, an unquenchable thirst, an innate longing. "No character, no deed, no work, ever yet satisfied us, that did not rise above mere utility into those harmonies and unities and sweetnesses that we call beautiful,"[53] Judd said.

Although the word "beautiful" expresses the whole of the deepest human feeling, no one can adequately define its nature. No doubt, Judd said, God made all things beautiful out of the exceeding beauty of his own nature. Man lives in an alabaster temple of earthly delights. "Darkness is beautiful, so is the storm; winter is beautiful in its high brilliancy, its wavy drifts, its starry flakes, in the moonlight flooding down the enamelled slopes."[54] Even heaven is "but the starry domes that overhangs our little faith and hope here; the bud and blossom of these germinant, terrestrial years; the Infinite, with white arms and golden crowns, welcoming the finite to a higher birth, into still higher realms of truth, goodness, and beauty."[55]

B. *"Language"*

Judd's lecture on "Language" was even more figuratively efflorescent, more poetically effervescent, more replete with high-flown oratorical flourishes than was "The Beautiful." Judd's thesis was that language was of divine origin:

> The original, divine words filled the great reservoir of human speech, which has been flowing down all the mountains and through all the valleys of human society; now throwing itself off in beautiful, many-tinted belles-lettres vapor; here taught by the poet to leap in jet, or pour in cascades; sometimes distilled by philosophers, sometimes muddied by boys; and in which, at last, Christianity itself is embodied, and descends as a dew and a rain upon the earth.[56]

There is something sublime, Judd continued, about words, perhaps something even awe-inspiring about the utterances beside the fireside, about the confidential whisper, about the eloquences of the forum, and about the words that ascend to the judgment seat of the Almighty. Language, an indestructible medium of human intercourse, connects man with the past and with God, who gave the language.

"Time was," Judd said, "when there were no words; when the universe, the sun and the stars, the shadowy grove, the whistling wind, the glancing brook, the playful fawn, the swift-winged bird, had no name; when all things were, in a sense, blank, devoid of interest; when, too, man with all his powers, was, as I think, utterly impotent to bestow these names."[57] Divine love granted man this power, and language has weathered all the vicissitudes of man's history. "It must, in the nature of things, have possessed considerable perfection, even in its incipiency and primitive use. Man could not invent it; God alone could give it."[58]

C. *"The Dramatic Element in the Bible"*

Judd's lectures on "The Beautiful" and "Language" were never published in their entirety, nor have the manuscripts been preserved. Miss Hall included generous extracts from these lectures from manuscripts she no doubt had in her possession at the time she was preparing her compilation of the *Life and Character of the Rev. Sylvester Judd.* She published in her book even more generous portions of Judd's lecture on "The Dramatic Element in the Bible." But in the case of this lecture, a manuscript of the complete lecture is in the Yale University Library. Across the top of the manuscript is written "Ms. of Sylvester Judd (Atlantic Monthly)." The interesting thing is that "The Dramatic Element in the Bible" was published in the August 1859 issue of the *Atlantic Monthly,* six and a half years after Judd's death. The lecture was published anonymously, and there is no indication anywhere in the issue that Judd was the author. The best guess is that Miss Hall, who had the manuscript in her possession, caused it to be published in the *Atlantic.* The fifty-two page manuscript was edited to hide the fact that it was originally written as a lecture; the "I's" of the manuscript were changed to less personal "we's"; some paragraphing and capitalization were changed; but the published article is a fair version of the original lecture. "The Dramatic Element in the Bible" is without the oratorical rhapsody of "Language." It is instead a rhetorical piece in the classical sense of being designed to persuade.

Judd wished to persuade his hearers that it was neither farfetched nor sacrilegious to seek "an artistical juxtaposition" between the representation and imitation of drama and the facts of biblical narrative. For instance, the distinguishing merit of Shakespeare, he argued, was his fidelity to Nature, but the Bible is equally true to Nature. Nothing holds up the mirror to life as does the Bible. Shakespeare also excelled in the delineation of character. "From the hand of Shakespeare, 'the lord and the tinker, the hero and the valet, come forth equally distinct and

clear.' In the Bible the various sorts of men are never
confounded, but have the advantage of being exhibited by
Nature herself, and not a contrivance of the imagination."
Human nature, in every stage of its development and in all of its
manifestations, is just as vividly set forth in Scripture as in
Shakespeare. Shakespeare, Judd said, makes one forget that a
man wrote the plays; in the Bible "the narrative of events
proceeds, for the most part, as if the author never existed."
Paraphrasing Coleridge, Judd said: "Shakespeare gives us no
moral highwaymen, no sentimental thieves and rat-catchers, no
interesting villians, no amiable adulteresses." Judd then commented: "The Bible goes even further than this, and is faithful to
the foibles and imperfections of its favorite characters, and
describes a rebellious Moses, a perjured David, a treacherous
Peter."[59]

After the Shakespeare prologue, Judd raised the curtain on
"the green, sunny garden of Eden, . . . which ever expresses the
bright dream of our youth, ere the rigor of misfortune or the
dulness of experience has spoilt it."[60] After running through the
drama in the Adam, Eve, and Serpent story, Judd mentioned the
story of Cain, the deception of Abraham, the story of Joseph, the
history of David, the deliverance of the Israelites from Egypt,
and so on. Judd's purpose was to illustrate by reference to
biblical narrative that the dialogue of the Bible has the charm of
poetry, that the Bible contains dramatic monologues as well as
dramatic episodes, and that the Bible illustrates the true object
of drama in its exhibition of human character.

Judd singled out some dramas based upon the Bible—Milton's
Samson Agonistes, Byron's *Cain,* and Hillhouse's *Hadad*—as
examples of literary treatments of biblical materials. The Book of
Job, the Song of Solomon, the Apocalypse of St. John were
conceived in a dramatic spirit, the lecturer asserted. And
mystery and morality plays of the Middle Ages were a "sort of
scenical illustration of the Sacred Scripture."[61] He concluded the
lecture with references to the drama inherent in the moving
episodes in the life of Christ. However, Judd gave the curtain
speech in his role as minister:

We speak of these things dramatically, but, after all, they are the
only great realities. Everything else is mimetic, phantasmal, tinkling.

Deeply do the masters of the drama move us; but the Gospel cleaves, inworks, regenerates. In the theatre, the leading characters go off in death and despair, or with empty conceits and forced frivolity; in the Gospel, tranquilly, grandly, they are dismissed to a serener life and a nobler probation. . . . The Gospel moves by, as a pure river of water of life, clear as a crystal, from the throne of God and the Lamb; on its surface play the sunbeams of hope; in its valleys rise the trees of life, beneath the shadows of which the weary years of human passion repose, and from the leaves of the branches of which is exhaled to the passing breeze healing for the nations.[62]

CHAPTER 3

Margaret, A Tale of the Real and Ideal *(1845)*

I   *The Inception*

O N July 4, 1841, Judd preached his sermon on "The Beautiful Zion" in which he set forth the aims of the Christian church as he saw them and his role as a Christian minister in accomplishing those aims.[1] That same day, having earlier determined that through fiction he would broaden his ministry far beyond the confines of his pulpit, Judd wrote to his father, the antiquarian and historian of the Connecticut Valley:

> I want very much that you should get for me any books published in this country during the last century, particularly after the close of the war; school-books, reading-books, primers, books of devotion, &c. &c. If you cannot get the books, get their names. I want to come at what may be styled an illustration of that period of the country,— 1783–1800. Dress, literature, &c. &c., the general costume of the time, what influences were upon it, its architecture, &c. The books that I want are mostly those that have perished, hence a difficulty. Also, if you could lay hands on any old arms, or bits of dress, any old furniture, &c. &c.[2]

Judd knew where to turn. No one was better qualified than his father to secure for him the specific background material he sought.[3]

But Judd wanted also to savor again at first hand the locale he had chosen for his story and to do some on-the-spot local-color investigation of his own. His trip this time down to Westhampton was to draw out of the older inhabitants of the area their recollections of the olden days. He reacquainted himself with the old store, the horse-sheds, and the meeting-house, reliving vicariously the stern Sabbath-keeping, the church-catechizing, and the hurrahing on the setting of the Sabbath sun. He visited Norwich Pond, the prototype of the Pond in *Margaret*, collecting there what information he could of an old herb doctress who once lived nearby. Judd found, too, according to Miss Hall, "some relics of a peculiarly marked people that used to inhabit the place, and took note of peculiar expressions made use of by them."[4] All aspects of the lore of the Westhampton-North-ampton-Norwich area interested him.

Back in Augusta, Judd made fresh excursions into Malta Woods to study the birds and the flora and the fauna. What he found there, he would weave into the fabric of *Margaret*. But it was not until sometime in 1843 that he began the arduous task of putting his novel together, the manuscript of which ultimately ran to over nine hundred pages.[5] On November 24, 1844, with an obvious sigh of relief, Judd wrote to his aunt Arethusa: "I finished my book last Friday. I have written on it till my hand is stiff, my eyes are sore, and my back aches. It has taken every leisure moment. I have not written a line to father, mother, brother, or sister, these months. I was resolved to finish that, before I did anything else."[6]

II   *The Publication*

On November 23, the day before his letter to Miss Hall, Judd posted a letter to the Boston publisher James Munroe:

Augusta, Nov. 23, 1844

Mr. Munroe,

Dear Sir,

I forward you today, by Child's Express, by way of Portland, a package, directed to "J. Munroe, care of James Munroe & Co" which is designed for yourself alone, and no other. I wish you to write me immediately on its arrival, that I may know it has arrived. In the letter that accompanies it, I did not say, that the matter is one that seems to me, on every account, to demand dispatch. The present would seem to be a favorable moment. Also, I wish to say, that if the package, is of no use to you, I wish you to return it to me immediately. Assure me also on the point of silence. Is the address of this letter the right one?

Yours &c,

S. Judd Jr.[7]

In an unsigned note that was obviously the preliminary draft of a reply to Judd, Munroe wrote:

[Boston, November 25, 1844]

Dear Sir[,]

Your letter was received by mail yesterday & by the Express today the package and letter came to hand safely[,] and as to the matter being kept a secret[,] you may rest assured that your name shall not be mentioned. I suppose your wish is that we publish the manuscript on our own account. Having already some ten or twelve vols in press and others contracted for[,] we could not undertake any other work at present were we ever so much inclined. I should prefer not to ask anyone to read over so voluminous a manuscript unless there was a prospect we should publish it. I will retain the manuscript in my desk until you give some direction concerning it, or if you wish to hand it to either of the person's named for perusal I will do so.[8]

Most of the correspondence that followed between the author and the publisher has been lost. However, two letters from Judd to Munroe, now in the Boston Public Library,[9] indicate that by spring the two were nearing terms for publication. On March 23, 1845, Judd inquired about binding, paper, and type. His brother James W. would aid in the sale of the novel, although he could not publish it.[10] On April 1, Judd wrote Munroe, stating his understanding of the terms of the contract and again reminding the publisher that he wished the author's name to be kept secret. But before the novel went to press, Munroe's firm was damaged by fire; and although Judd's manuscript was spared, Munroe now decided against publishing it. Jordan and Wiley agreed to take it and in August 1845 brought out an edition of one thousand copies, with the anonymous author assuming half of the expense of publication.

III   *The Purpose*

In his 460-page romance—*Margaret. A Tale of the Real and Ideal, Blight and Bloom; Including Sketches of a Place Not Before Described, Called Mons Christi*—Judd had fashioned a didactic tale to display what he conceived to be the errors of a false theology, the evils of intemperance, the mischief inherent in military training, the unjust treatment of the Indian, the inhumane treatment of prisoners, the horrors of capital punishment, and the wrong education of children. Here was Judd the Unitarian author in his role as reformer, a role Judd says in *Philo* that the serious professional man can hardly avoid.

But his purpose was not to write a jeremiad; and even before the book came from the press, Judd felt the need to rehearse to a kindred soul his purpose and hopes for the novel. On July 15, he wrote his friend in Worcester, the Reverend Edward Everett Hale:

> The book designs to promote the course of liberal Christianity, or, in other words, of a pure Christianity: it would give body and soul to the divine elements of the gospel. . . . Its basis is Christ: him it would restore to the church, him it would develop in the soul, him it would enthrone in the world. . . . In its retrospective aspect, it seeks to preserve some reminiscences of the age of our immediate fathers, thereby describing a period of which we have no enduring monuments, and one the traces of which are fast evanescing. The book makes a large account of nature, the birds and flowers, for the sake of giving greater individuality to, and bringing into stronger relief, that which the religious mind passes over too loosely and vaguely. It is a New England book, and is designed to embody the features and improve the character of our favored region.
>
> But more particularly, let me say, the book seems fitted to fill a gap, long left open in Unitarian literature,—that of imaginative writings. The Orthodox enjoy the works of Bunyan, Hannah More, Charlotte Elizabeth, the Abbots, &c, &c.[11] But what have we in their place? The original design of the book was solely to occupy this niche; although, I fancy, you may think it has somewhat passed these limits. . . . My own personal education in, and acquaintance with, "Orthodoxy," as well as my idea of the prevalent errors of the age, lead me to think such a book is needed. . . . The author wishes to hasten what are believed to be the peculiar triumphs of Christianity.[12]

The genesis of *Margaret* may well have been in an experience which Judd related in one of his letters to W——n in his *A Young*

Man's Account of His Conversion from Calvinism. At a time
when he was struggling with some particularly vexing
metaphysical problem, he was diverted by the sight of a little
girl, probably his little sister Pin, frolicking in the freedom and
glee of youth. Of her he wrote:

She was in the incipient development of her primitive being. She had
not experienced, so far as I know, a change from what was her original
nature. I called her attention, and read to her the verse, "Blessed are
the pure in heart," and so forth, and asked her if she thought it was
good in God to bless only those who had pure hearts. "Oh!" said she, "I
wish my heart to be always pure." Then she added, with a look
between a smile and a thought, such as you sometimes see pass over the
face of a child, "I should not be happy in Heaven with God, if I had a
wicked heart." All the world may not perceive the bearing of this slight
occurrence. You will understand me when I say it was a hint, a blessed
hint, to better things.[13]

Margaret is the development of that hint, especially in "Part I."
The nature of the child was central in any theological discussion.
Judd settled for himself this vexing question, and *Margaret*
became the dramatization of that conclusion. Judd's child-
centered church was an attempt to put it into practice.

IV   The Plot

A. *"Part I. Childhood"*

Judd's *Bildungsroman,* with its three-part division, has a linear
structure which begins with Margaret, the universal child, and
ends with Margaret, the idealized woman. In "Part I. Childhood," the universal child is introduced by means of what Judd
called a "phantasmagorical perspective." The babe could have
been born anywhere—on the Thames, in the Amazon, or in
Mississippi. It could have been born to anyone—to Queen
Victoria or Sally Twig. It could have been Caucasian, Mongolian,
American, Ethiopian, or Malay. Conditions of birth made no
difference, for it was God's own child as all children are, a
marvel of creation. "The Spirit of the Eternal, that blows
everywhere, has animated its soul. . . . It is a miracle of the All-
working, it is endowed by the All-gifted . . .; the inspiration of
the Almighty hath given it understanding. It will look after God,

its Maker, by how many soever names he may be called; it will aspire to the Infinite . . . ; it will seek to know the truth; it will long to be loved; it will sin and be miserable; if it has none to care for it, it will die."[14] In this statement is the outline of "Part I. Childhood."

The Margaret of the story, however, is a New England child, selected from among all the world's Margarets. As her story opens, she is a nine-year-old child, industrious, given to dreaming, living close to nature, and growing up by the Pond, a body of water obviously symbolic of the eternal. The Pond, the author noted, "was commonly reported to have no bottom, and it possesses the minds of the people with a sort of indefinable awe: but this Margaret was too young to feel; she took manifest delight in skimming across that dark, deep mystery."[7] In time, she would fathom the depths of its symbolic meaning.

Judd placed Margaret in a family that seemed anything but promising in the proper rearing of a child. This, of course, was done to show that the child—far from being a depraved being— could preserve its pristine, heaven-born qualities even in the face of earth-born pressures. Pluck Hart, the head of the household, was a hard-drinking, irreverent, law-defying man. His wife, Brown Moll, was a fit companion. The couple had three sons—Nimrod, who was away from home, Hash, who farmed his father's land, and Chilion, who was fond of rustic music. They were an uncouth bunch, often little removed from outright vulgarity. The family, popularly known as the Indians, lived by the Pond in the West District outside the village of Livingston.

Margaret's assistant in her nature study was Obed, the only child of Widow Wright, the herb doctress of the community and, along with Master Elliman, one of Judd's successful comic creations in the novel. Margaret had to be made to realize, however, that all that she saw in nature did not constitute all that was real, so Judd had her join her brother Chilion and Obed in a bee-hunt. She was appalled at seeing the bees suffocate from the smoke; she had eaten honey, but she had never before associated the honey with the death of the bees. The novelist then interjected: "What is the child's first sense of death? She would have given all her little heart was worth, could she restore the life she had so thoughtlessly taken, and see them again busy, blithe, happy about her house. Tears ran down her cheeks, the unconscious expiation of Nature to the Infinite Life"(19). Heaven was about her and over her, but she lived in a real world of cruelty and death.

Bartholomew Elliman—the schoolmaster or the Master, as he was generally called—was a prolix buffoon, yet a carefully conceived and skillfully drawn one. Margaret was a favorite of his, but even for him she would not drink pupelo when he visited the Harts. *Something*—she knew not what at the time—would not let her. Yet Margaret was such a dutiful, such an obedient child in other circumstances, that she gave up her precious spelling book in order to obtain rum for the Harts; she knew her sacrifice would please them. She pleased others, not herself, by finding water through her remarkable powers with the witch hazel stick.

Nimrod, volatile by nature, was a swashbuckling, restless, but good-hearted rogue, who came back to Livingston once a year to the consternation of the villagers. As a boy, he had been apprenticed to a blacksmith, but such work was hardly compatible with his temperament. In time, he became a hostler, bartender, errand boy, and serving man to a lady. While still in his teens, he joined a military detachment to defend the northern frontiers, but deserted to Canada instead and joined a band of smugglers operating on the eastern seaboard. In New York, Nimrod met a Mr. Girardeau, a late eighteenth-century Shylock, a fear-ridden, superstitious merchant, whose daughter had eloped with a foreigner. Taking the name Foxly, Nimrod left the smugglers and signed on in the service of the merchant. Nimrod was warned to have nothing to do with the wayward daughter. "She has married to her own shame, and my grief. I have borne with her, till forebearance becomes a sin. She would strip me of my possessions. The author of her degradation she would make the pandar to her cruelty. I am doubly beset, they are in a conspiracy against me. Heed not her, listen not to her importunity, let her suffer. I have no feelings of a father; they have been wrenched and torn away; I cannot own a viper for a child"(61). But Nimrod did not believe his employer, and he set out to find the truth for himself about Jane Girardeau and the foreigner.

Using the flashback technique, Judd related the touchingly sentimental story of Gottfried Brückmann and Jane Girardeau, which even his severest critics acknowledged to be well told. In it, Judd demonstrated that he could write in a sentimental mode. Brückmann, a Hessian mercenary during the Revolutionary War, sought in every way possible to avoid being drafted into the service of the British Crown. He fled into the Hartz Mountains. "Whatever of romance, literature, poetry, descended into the mass of the population; whatever of legendary tale or cabalistic observance was cherished by the common heart; whatever of imaginative temper, ideal aspiration, or mystic enthusiasm has ever characterized any portion of his countrymen, Brückmann possessed" (62). There in the Hartz Mountains, among the cloud-piercing hills, lakes embosomed in mountains, waterfalls, gorgeous sunsets, dense and fantastic fogs, and perennial snows, Brückmann, the schoolmaster, fell in love with Margaret Bruneau, one of his pupils. But in the midst of the beautiful love affair, Brückmann was seized by the authorities, forcibly taken to Rotterdam, and shipped off to America. Before the war was over, however, Brückmann heard of Margaret's death; and any appeal his native country might otherwise have held for him vanished.

The war over, Brückmann decided to stay in New York. "Contrary to the usual maxim, he loved those whom he had injured, and was willing that whatever of life or energy remained to him should be given to the Americans" (63). He would teach French, but there were few who wanted to study the language. So, sick at heart, he sat by his window and made music on his flute. Jane Girardeau heard the music; her father sensed her interest in the music and her curiosity about the musician; and he ordered her to stay in her room at night, but she would not. This was not the first time the willful girl had disobeyed her tyrannical father. "Like the hidden fires of the earth she broke out whenever she could find vent. She was held down, not subdued. She was too elastic to flatten, too spiritual to stagnate" (65).

Jane, without her father's knowledge, enrolled as one of Brückmann's few students; and she made no secret to him of her interest in him and in the story of his past. His account of his love for the lost Margaret fascinated her. Jane asked all the usual feminine questions; especially she wanted to know why Brückmann loved her. "She was," Brückmann told Jane on one occasion, "a transparent, articulate revelation of God" (67). In visions, Margaret had, he said, at times come to him; but now "You have revived those visions, and refreshing communions,"

(67) he said to Jane. Brückmann's abiding love for Margaret only made him purer, diviner in Jane's eyes. Jane, in her mind, entered the delightful company, became one of the glorious trio, and saw herself fulfilled and symbolized in Margaret.

The vengeful Girardeau succeeded in having Brückmann clapped into jail for debt, but the resourceful Jane succeeded in getting in to see him. She declared that she could not live without him. "You have," she said, "given back to my soul the only answer it ever received; . . . You have introduced me to the participation of yourself and Margaret; you have inspired me with a desire to know more of the laws of the spirit's life" (69). Jane proposed marriage to Brückmann and urged him to tell her ever more about Margaret. "I will grow up into her image; I will transmute myself to her nature. You shall have a double Margaret; no, not double, but one. Nay, if needs be, I will go out of myself; I will be the servant of you both. Call me your child, yours and Margaret's child, your spirit child, and so love me" (70).

Jane paid Brückmann's debts and secured his release. They were married. In six months Brückmann fell ill, but not before the couple knew that a little Margaret was on the way. It was at this point, when Jane came to her father's house for clothes, that Nimrod found out who the wayward daughter was. Her father informed Nimrod that Jane was about to have a child that could prove a great injury to him and to Nimrod as well. Curious, Nimrod sought out Jane and the dying Brückmann; touched, he befriended the appealing couple and promised Jane, who had a premonition that her own end was near, that the unborn child would be named Margaret and that he would personally see that it was taken in safety to the Pond, where the little Margaret would be reared as his own sister. Thus, when the old merchant ordered Nimrod to get rid of the child, Nimrod carried out to the letter his promise to Jane.

The second half of "Part I. Childhood"—from Chapter 13 on—is devoted, sometimes in a broadly comic style, to Margaret's growing up and acquiring knowledge of the world and of spiritual matters. She attended a militia day and enjoyed the pomp until she saw the cruelty meted out to those who disobeyed the officers and the drunkenness that followed the exercises. And for the first time in her life, Margaret had a sense of danger. Shortly thereafter, for the first time, she attended a church service. On the way, she picked flowers for a jailed murderer, but the jailer would not let her give them to him since prisoners were not to be spoken to on the Lord's Day. After the meeting, Margaret—understanding little of what was said to her—was urged to take Christ as her atoning sacrifice; but, with her own childlike logic, she reasoned that she need not fear a God that would not punish the grasshoppers who broke the Sabbath by playing.

Margaret, after a day about the Pond and its mysterious depths, had a dream in which she saw a cross planted in the ground, where it put forth leaves and flowers and on the top of which a milk-white dove alighted. The dove flew to Margaret's shoulder, an act, she felt, which established a relationship between her and the two men she saw about the cross. Margaret, in her dream, picked some berries and flowers for the Beautiful One. The people Margaret had seen at church gathered about the two figures, Christ and John the Apostle, unsure, however, whether or not any of them were worthy partakers of the efficacy of Christ's death. The Apostle declared that no human being was sinful by nature and that even deep love in the soul would remove whatever traces there were of the carnal mind. Jesus invited all to come to him, for he had come to save, not condemn. Salvation, he said, was a divine union with God and Christ. Turning to Margaret, Christ said, "Be pure in heart and you shall see God. Love much, and he shall be manifest to you. Your flowers are fair, your spirit fairer. . . . The Church has fallen. The Eve of Religion has again eaten the forbidden fruit. You shall be a co-worker with me in its second redemption. I speak to you in parables, you understand not. You shall understand at another day" (110).

Margaret, eager to understand the Infinite, appealed to the Master. Though full of erudition—or perhaps because of it—he could not help her. Judd's point seems to be that a knowledge of God is not attained through worldly wisdom. The Master, in fact, was a selfish person who often made use of Margaret to search out the woods for wild flowers he wanted. "She found varieties of fungus, yellow, scarlet, and blood-colored, which she tore from the sides of trees, from stumps and rails. She gathered the wild columbine, snake-root, red cohosh, purple bush-trefoil, flaxbell-flower, the beautiful purple orchis, and dodder, that gay yellow-liveried parasite" (123).

On one such excursion, Margaret and her dog Bull were surprised by a tornado. "It leaped like a maniac from the skies, and with a breadth of some twenty rods and an extent of four or five miles, swept everything in its course; the forest was mown down before it, orchard-trees were torn up by the roots, large rocks unearthed, chimneys dashed to the ground, roofs of houses whirled into the air, fences scattered, cows lifted from their feet, sheep killed, the strongest fabrics of man and nature driven about like stubble" (127).

When Margaret recovered, she found herself covered with debris. Bull had fled; the paths were obliterated. Exhausted and bleeding, she sought shelter under a large rock. Switching to a storybook mode and style, Judd then told the story of Margaret and the four bears, a fanciful tale that seems out of place among the other episodes of Margaret's developing awareness of the real:

She had not been sitting long when she saw approaching the same place a large, shaggy, black bear, with three cubs. The bear looked at Margaret, and Margaret looked at the bear. "It is very strange," the old bear seemed to say; the little bears frisked about as if they thought it was funny to see a little two-legged child in their bed. Margaret sat very still and said nothing, only she wished she could tell the bears how tired she was, and hoped they wouldn't take offense at her being there. The big bear came close to her hand, and even licked the blood that flowed from her arm; and Margaret went so far as to stroke the long brown nose of the bear, and was no more afraid than if it had been her own Bull. The motherly beast seemed to be thinking, "How bad I should feel if it had been one of the cubs that was hurt!" Then she lay on the ground, and the little bears knew supper was ready. Now the old bear saw that Margaret was tired and bruised, and must have felt that she was hungry also, for she gave a sort of wink with her eyes that seemed to say, "Won't you take a seat at our table, too? It is the best I can set, for, as you see, I haven't any hands, and can't use spoons." It would have been ungrateful in Margaret not to accept so kind an invitation. Finally, the good dam and her young and Margaret all cuddled down together, and were soon asleep; only one of the little bears could not get to sleep so easily for thinking what a strange bedfellow he had, and he got up two or three times just to look at the child. (128)

Meanwhile, the news of the tornado reached the Pond; and

when Margaret did not return, Chilion and Bull, who had found his way back home, set out to find her, but failed. The news reached Livingston, and the entire population went into action. The Master was one of the first to come near the spot where Margaret sang to the entranced bears. The mother bear and her cubs, shocked out of their song-induced trance, gave chase, and the frightened man ran through the woods, crying, "Ursa major! Ursae minores! Great Bear! Little Bear! O!" (132). The other men rushed to Margaret's side, and they carried her back to the village. Like Spenser's Una, her beauty had tamed the wild beast.

Judd ended "Part I" with something approaching a prose poem to winter, proving that his forte was in description, not in narrative conception or execution.

B. *"Part II. Youth"*

Margaret, now a serious pupil of the Master, was in her mid-teens when "Part II. Youth" opened, but her studies did not keep her from participating in the annual chores, such as maple sugar making, or from scouring the woods in search of rare plants, or from the thrill of listening to the birds in sylvan concert. One day, while walking among the trees, Margaret, reminiscent of Coleridge's Christabel, heard a sound issuing from the shady side of a pine tree. There, stripping the bright buds from the branches of the Judas tree and uttering plaintive sounds, Margaret saw a delicate lady. The lady, who wished to be called Rose, was in despair because she, in a moment of weakness, had succumbed to the wiles of a seducer. Margaret determined to restore Rose to a sense of spiritual well-being and to physical health.

In the meantime, the Master secured a post at the village school for Margaret; but because she refused to teach from the religiously slanted primer and would not use the birch, she was soon dismissed. On her way back to the Pond, she was accosted by a handsome young man with dark, piercing eyes and an affectionate expression who called himself Mr. Anonymous. A few days later, he showed up at the Pond, but had eyes only for Margaret. Claiming he adored her, he attempted to force his attentions on her. Margaret threatened to jump into the Pond, but was saved from doing so by the timely arrival of Obed.

Margaret's encounter with the sensuous Mr. Anonymous served as a contrasting backdrop for the true love affair that was soon to develop between Margaret and Mr. Evelyn.

Just as the Master was her instructor in worldly knowledge, Mr. Evelyn became Margaret's spiritual mentor. Like Mr. Anonymous, Mr. Evelyn, too, appeared at the Pond. He found Margaret poring over a theological book. She wanted to know who God was. Mr. Evelyn suggested that she seek an answer from the church people, but she replied that their thoughts only ran to sin, sinners, the Fall, recovery, justification, election, depravity, hell, damnation, and so on. When Mr. Evelyn spoke of Christ, Margaret recognized him as the Beautiful One of her dream.

In a lengthy climactic chapter, Judd had Mr. Evelyn instruct Margaret fully in all matters of theology, so fully that, at the end of the chapter, Margaret exclaimed, "You have said the last word; I have no more questions" (227). God, he told her, was the Soul of all, the supreme Intelligence, the uncreated Creator, and the invisible Seer. God it was who breathed into man the breath of life, thus providing man with a soul as ever-living as the Divinity himself. Christ was given the problems of man, God, and the universe to resolve, and with divine assistance he did so. Christ came to redeem man from "war, intemperance, slavery, unkindness, . . . bigotry, irreligion, pious frauds, persecution, simony, burglary, peculation, treason, perjury, kidnapping, piracy, scandal, ingratitude, intrigue, bribery, meanness, social inequality, governmental misrule, spirit of caste, oppression of labor, [and] superciliousness" (214). The fundamental reason for sin was that man ceased to love God, thus losing the image of God within. However, Mr. Evelyn assured her, man's natural susceptibility to goodness and truth can never be extinguished. Man is a partaker of the Divine Nature through Christ, the Moral Revelation of God. Faith would be taking Christ to herself. "Christ shall preside over us," Margaret exclaimed. "I will worship him. . . . But the names must be changed. Bacchus Hill shall be Christ's Hill, Orpheus's Pond, his Pond. He shall be supreme; Head, Pond, and all, shall hence forth be called Mons Christi" (227). Christ's statement in "Part I" that Margaret would understand fully at a later time was now fulfilled.

From this point on in "Part II," Judd sets a two-fold task for himself—to show, in an episodic way, Margaret, the maturing Christian, meeting the temptations of life, facing with Christian courage the trials of life, and shaping a satisfying life for herself; and to tie up the various strands of his narrative into a neat bundle. Margaret supplied the sympathic love Rose needed and discovered that a rake named Raxman was the Mr. Anonymous who seduced Rose and attacked her. Margaret's brother Chilion was wrongly accused of murder following a drunken orgy that began as a husking bee, and she suffered the torments of his undeserved execution. After that ordeal, Margaret and Rose took a trip to Boston, Hartford, New York, and Baltimore, where Margaret worshiped in the famous churches. In New York, through the help of the Jones family, Margaret met her grandfather. The senile old man put his hand on her head and muttered, "Jane, Jane, my own Jane, my Jane's own!" (325). Judd ended "Part II" with "The History of Mr. Girardeau." In a set of unnecessary coincidences, it is revealed to the reader that Brown Moll was really Mr. Girardeau's niece and that Raxman was his grand-nephew. The old man was, of course, repentant for all the evil he had perpetrated.

C. *"Part III. Woman"*

The short "Part III. Woman" consists of a series of familiar letters, often chatty, written, with one exception, from Mons Christi by Margaret to Anna Jones, a friend she made in New York, and by Rose to various members of the Jones family. The purpose of "Part III" is obviously to suggest a blueprint for an ideal social order and to picture the fulfillment of Christ's prophecy that Margaret would be a coworker with him in the church's second redemption. The letters indicate that Rose, now restored to spiritual and physical health, is romantically inter-ested in Edward Jones, a young minister, and that there was developing between them a relationship much akin to that earlier described between Margaret and Mr. Evelyn. In fact, Mr. Evelyn himself was soon to return from abroad, and a double wedding was a distinct possibility.

Margaret and Mr. Evelyn were married and set about acquiring all of Mons Christi, where they wished to build a church to be called Christ Church. Rose and Edward Jones, too, married, and Edward became the minister of the new church.

Mr. Evelyn had brought from Europe a valuable library and a few choice pieces of sculpture to go with the statues of Peace, Truth, Faith, Hope, Love, and Beauty that already adorned Mons Christi. And extensive orchards were planted and stocked with native birds.

A new moral tone began to permeate the area. Edward Jones preached against intemperance; the new merchant would keep no ardent spirits; the old still was turned into a barn; and four distilleries ceased operation. The new jail had good beds, books, lights, a looking-glass, a wash-stand, a flower vase, and green blinds. Despite such luxuries, recommitments to the jail became few and far between. Military training-days were abolished. Mons Christi had music; it had its Chilion Band. "Have we not here," Margaret wrote Anna, "what his grace the Duke of Devonshire might envy? pleasure-grounds, rich meadows, the embellishment of a full-grown plantation, beautiful lawns, many a paddock" (352).

In another letter to Anna, Margaret wrote: "The end of my being is accomplished! The prophecy of my life is fulfilled. My dreams have gone out in realities. The Cross Is Erected on Mons Christi!" (353). The Sabbaths became days of liberty, rest, and recreation. The communion celebrated the day when Christ would perfectly come in the souls of men over all the earth. The church instituted a number of festival days, twelve in all, to go along with the secular celebrations, such as the May-pole, May dances, and the Queen of May. All Christian churches in the area enjoyed fellowship together.

To conclude his novel, Judd had Mr. Evelyn in a letter to Anna write an encomium on Margaret, and Margaret in a letter to Anna described once more the present glories and the future prospects of Mons Christi. Mr. Evelyn maintained that Margaret, under God and in Christ, was the soul of Mons Christi, translating Nature to man and man to himself. She had an intuitive perception of the law by which all things—physical, moral, and religious—gravitate toward a common center and coalesce into one. There was a correspondence between her soul and the Soul of all things. Nature, therefore, was Margaret teaching by example. From her earliest childhood, Margaret "courted alliance with an imperishable Nature" (379). But Christ gave her her knowledge. However, in her letter to Anna, Margaret maintained that it was Mr. Evelyn who revealed Christ to her. And regardless of the role Mr. Evelyn assigned to Margaret in the conception and building of Mons Christi, a modest Margaret would have it that she and all the others were simply coworkers with God. She did, however, glory in Mons Christi's success, arguing that much of it was due to the power of Beauty over the common mind and the providing of wholesome recreation, "another distinct and stringent law of God and Nature" (392). Presidents Adams and Jefferson came to see the wonders of Mons Christi and stayed to praise.

V   *The Critics*

Judd was keenly aware of the critical reception of *Margaret* and particularly sensitive to the adverse criticism his novel received. He collected the critical notices and carefully pasted them in a notebook now among the Judd Papers at Harvard.[15] On August 9, 1845, the *Boston Daily Advertiser* called *Margaret* "quite a remarkable book . . . [but with] much of extravagance and caricature in some parts of the book." The *Christian Register* for September 6 also found it remarkable. "There is," the reviewer said, "an originality, a freedom of style, a beauty and depth of sentiment, and a fulness of delineation in his book, which are peculiar in their kind and not often equalled." Charles K. Whipple reviewed *Margaret* for the September 26 issue of the *Liberator*. After commenting on the author's rare and remarkable cast of mind and his rare and peculiar attainment, he said the novel showed "a wonderfully minuté acquaintance with the language, manners, customs, virtues, vices, and daily household life of the country-people of New England at the time of the Revolution." On September 1, Margaret Fuller noticed the novel in the *New York Tribune,* but admitted later that she had not read the novel at the time. Once she got around to reading it, she amended her earlier comments in a review published on January 10, 1846, seeing the novel then as a "work full of genius, profound in its meaning, and of admirable fidelity to Nature and its details." She found the book an "auspicious omen, that an American literature is possible even in our day." The *Bangor Daily Whig and Courier,* five days later, quoted Miss Fuller, "the female assistant editor of the New York *Tribune,*" and

announced that the work was said to be by the Reverend Mr.
Judd of Augusta. Judd must have been particularly pleased with
the comment of his hometown newspaper. The novel was, the
Northampton Democrat said on June 23, "a beautiful allegory,
containing the highest inspiration of Christianity."

A. *Frederic Dan Huntington*

The full-length reviews in the journals—with a few notable
exceptions—were written by Judd's fellow Unitarian ministers,
men from whom Judd had a right, he felt, to expect understanding and acceptance of his work. But, at best, the reviews were
mixed. For instance, Frederic Dan Huntington, who grew up just
across the Connecticut River from Northampton and who was a
fellow divinity student with Judd at Harvard, reviewed the novel
for the November 1845 issue of the *Christian Examiner*. After
noting that the novel was in three parts, he said that "the first of
these might have been withheld from the printer without
essentially diminishing the value of the whole; or at least it might
have been advantageously compressed into half a dozen pages. It
abounds in dull and diffuse details of persons and things that
possess few claims to the reader's attention, and some of which
make but a small figure in the narrative. It is encumbered with
dialogue of low life conducted without that humor, raciness, and
spirit, which alone can make such conversation otherwise than
tedious, if not quite revolting."[16] Huntington did see, however,
'the episode relating to Brückmann . . . [as] a happy instance of
feeling delicately managed,"[17] but the novel as a whole, as a
viable romance, he found barely more than respectable. The
novel, however, did betray the author's "genuine love for his
race, and a hearty desire to serve well the interest of
humanity."[18] Huntington, the minister, did find the chapter on
"Christianity," in which Mr. Evelyn fully instructed Margaret in
the truths of Christianity, to be "full of eloquence and power and
truth. We do not often meet with," he wrote, "finer illustrations
and statements of the nature, character and real mission of
Christ, and the significance of the Gospel."[19] Huntington too was
impressed with Margaret's letters in "Part III." "They show," he
said, "how the kingdom of Christ veritably comes on earth,"[20] a
statement that should have particularly pleased Judd.

B. W. B. O. Peabody

William Bourne Oliver Peabody, a Harvard Doctor of Divinity (1842) and an acknowledged authority on ornithology, was settled over the Unitarian church in Springfield, Massachusetts. He wrote the thirty-nine-page review of *Margaret* which appeared in the January 1846 issue of the *North American Review*. In Peabody's view, *Margaret* was everything a novel should not be. A novel should have "a richness of attainment, a cheerful and sympathetic spirit, a wide-reaching mastery of style, together with a clear and strong good sense"[21] which *Margaret* did not have. The doctrine itself was enough to "crash down the novel with its own weight";[22] and when the object is to set forth and sustain new theories of social reorganization, the difficulty is even greater: the novel is no place to convince one of Utopian schemes. Peabody did not agree that children, left in their pristine purity, would be better off than those who were instructed in religious matters.

And why did authors go out of their way to make New England seem so desperately vulgar? "In the name of common sense," Peabody wrote, "is it true, that there is nobody but Sam Slick extant in this part of the habitable globe?"[23] The reviewer found Judd's view of society to be "not only dreary and disgusting, but one-sided and unjust; it is not drawn from the living reality of those times, but from a theoretical imagination of what, in his view, they are likely to have been."[24]

Peabody was also piqued at what he called a sort of cant Judd had fallen into: Judd's angry lamentation over the fallen church. Peabody also attacked the impracticality of reformers, of which Judd was obviously one. Peabody admitted, though, that there was no power sufficient to bring about reform except that found in Christianity. But Judd was a misled visionary: his idea was that, if Christianity "can be set free from the corruptions which retain its energies, and brought into direct communication with human hearts, it will bring their powers and affections into full and harmonious action."[25] While this may be true, it was not clear to the reviewer "that the want of power is owing to the particular form in which the religion manifests itself, nor that it would become efficient at once if its forms of doctrine or service were altered."[26]

Admitting that the novelist had an unusual knack at describing natural scenery and in representing New England manners of an age gone by, Peabody found the novel, however, lacking as a finished literary work. The characters were not consistent throughout; the style ranged from "rich and expressive" to "slovenly, snappish, and jerking"; and the novel was "unequal, disjointed, and full of contrasts and contradictions."[27]

C. *Dexter Clapp*

Though not altogether favorable, the review that came to Judd's attention that he most appreciated was one written by the Reverend Dexter Clapp of the small Unitarian enclave in New Orleans. Clapp, a native of Northampton and an early school-mate of Judd, had no idea who the author of *Margaret* was when his fifteen-page review was published in the April 1846 issue of the *Southern Quarterly Review*. Clapp repeated Margaret Fuller's contention that *Margaret* "leads us to believe in the possibility of a distinctive American Literature."[28] He antici-pated James Russell Lowell's observation when he said that "it will be called the Yankee novel, and rightly; for no where else have we seen the thought, dialect and customs of a New England village so well and faithfully represented."[29] Clapp was quick, however, to point out that his praise was not unqualified: the novel had excess of coloring, ludicrous excesses, more caricature than truth and reality, some vulgarities that could be justified only on the basis that they were no doubt true, and exaggerations of good and evil that went beyond what they appeared to be to the outward senses. Clapp, however, placed the author of *Margaret* in the same category as Dickens, Carlyle, and Frederika Bremer, but only because he had clearly in mind a moral idea that directed his course. It was his excellent motive that redeemed his bad taste, for bad taste he exhibited in presenting aspects of common life in an offensively vulgar way. "In criticism," Clapp wrote, "offenses against taste are almost as obnoxious as those against virtue."[30] Clapp saw in the author of *Margaret*, though, uncommon gifts which, if properly harnessed, may give him a distinguished name in literature and reform.

The style of the book, Clapp wrote, was original. That, however, was not to be taken to mean that the style was altogether commendable. There were too many uncouth words and unnecessary sprinklings of words from various languages, especially in the speech of Master Elliman. Yet there were examples of great descriptive beauty where the author demonstrated a keen ear for the melody of language. "That is a good style, which conveys most forcibly and completely an author's idea,"[31] Clapp said. The style of *Margaret* did not sufficiently meet this criterion.

But there were a lot of good things to be said about the book. No work of fiction that had appeared in America, in Clapp's view, was of more significance than *Margaret*. The author was a bold prophet of the age—a bold prophet of the future—who predicted that out of the incompatible elements of the New World would emerge a harmony that would elevate the natural and spiritualize daily experiences. As a romance, Clapp found the novel "very imperfect, little more than respectable, but as a record of great ideas and pure sentiments, we place it among the few great books of the age."[32] Clapp agreed with the novelist that the individual heart needed regeneration, and so did society. Perfect men and women were possible only in a perfect society. A perfect society in its true state was one in which the impulses and interests of each man were in harmony with those of all men and those of all men in harmony with those of each individual, Clapp observed.

D. *Orestes Brownson*

A review of a different sort came from Orestes Brownson, then in his Roman Catholic phase. In an article entitled "Protestantism Ends in Transcendentalism" in the July 1846 issue of *Brownson's Quarterly Review*, Brownson admitted that much of what he knew about *Margaret* was second-hand. Nevertheless, he knew enough, he felt, to label the book Transcendental, with all that that implied.[33] Judd was even, Brownson said, a successful minister of the latest form of Protestantism. Mons Christi, according to Brownson, represented the human heart, and Christ represented man's higher or instinctive nature, a nature which, if listened to, would lead man to know and obey all that Christ taught. Thus Margaret was "represented as possessing in herself all the elements of the most perfect Christian character, and as knowing by heart all the essential principles of Christian faith and morals."[34] Judd, Brownson wrote, settled upon love as the

great teacher and decided that the true method of education was
to have the pupil fall in love with the tutor or the tutor with the
pupil. "Whence it follows, that it is a great mistake to suppose it
desirable or even proper that tutor and pupil should both be of
the same sex."[35] Brownson concluded that the genus of the book,
if not the species, would merit the Transcendental label. And if
he had sufficient time to go into the licentiousness and
blasphemy of the novel, he felt he might even definitely
determine its species. As a parting shot, Brownson said: "But this
must suffice; and when we add that the author seems to comprise
in himself several species at once, besides the whole genus
humbuggery, we may dismiss the book with sincere pity for him
who wrote it, and a real prayer for his speedy conversion,
through grace, to that Christianity which was given to man from
above, and not, spider-like, spun out of his own bowels."[36]

E. *Margaret Fuller*

The most fully appreciative and flattering comments Judd may
have read came from the pens of Margaret Fuller and James
Russell Lowell. Margaret Fuller in her essay entitled "American
Literature: Its Position in the Present Time, and Prospects for
the Future," published in 1846 in her *Papers on Literature and
Art,* wrote of *Margaret:*

It is a work of great power and richness, a genuine disclosure of the life
of mind and the history of character. Its descriptions of scenery and the
common people, in the time and place it takes up, impart to it the
highest value as a representative of transient existence which had a
great deal of meaning. The beautiful simplicity of action upon and
within the mind of Margaret, Heaven lying so clearly about her in her
infancy, of the hut of drunkards, the woods, the village, and their
ignorant, simple human denizens; her unconscious growth to the stature
of womanhood, the flow of life impelled by her, the spiritual
intimations of her dreams; the prophecies of music in the character of
Chilion; the naive discussion of the leading reform movements of the
day in their rudimentary forms; the archness, the humor, the profound
religious faith, make of this book an aviary from which doves shall go
forth to discover and report of all the green spots of promise in the
land. Of books like this, as good and still better, our new literature shall
be full; and though one swallow does not make a summer, yet we greet
in this one "Yankee novel" the sufficient earnest of riches that only

need the skill of competent miners to be made current for the benefit of man.[37]

F. *James Russell Lowell*

James Russell Lowell, in a review of Longfellow's *Kavanagh: A Tale* in the *North American Review* for July 1849, like Margaret Fuller, called for a distinctly American literature, a literature national to the extent of being free from outworn conventionalities, yet humane and manly enough to match the American political experiment. "The story of 'Margaret,'" he wrote, "is the most emphatically *American* book every written."[38] Excusing the faults of *Margaret*, Lowell said: "The want of plan and slovenliness of construction are characteristics of a new country. The scenery, characters, dialect, and incidents mirror New England life as truly as Fresh Pond reflects the sky. The moral, also, pointing forward to a new social order, is the intellectual antitype of that restlessness of disposition, and facility of migration which are among our chief idiosyncrasies. The mistake of our imaginative writers generally is that, though they may take an American subject, they *costume* it in a foreign or antique fashion. The consequence is a painful vagueness and unreality."[39] Such was not the case with *Margaret*, Lowell argued.

VI   *Judd's Defense*

Judd felt a need to answer the most stinging of the criticisms leveled at him and his novel. The opportunity came when Phillips, Sampson and Company published a two-volume, revised edition of *Margaret* in 1851. The authorship of *Margaret* was no longer a secret. Judd included the "Author's Note," dated Riverside, Augusta, May 12, 1851, as a kind of preface to the revised edition. He had no apologies to offer, he pointed out, for the ideas presented in *Margaret* or his object in writing the book. He did, however, want to reply to four specific charges:

First, "'He is too minute; he seems to be making out a ship's manifest, instead of telling a plain story'" (iv). Judd's defense was that he had watched every bird, hunted every flower, and trodden every footpath mentioned in the book. Of course, no author should expect the public to look with favor on his own recreations, but an author might expect the public to be charitable toward the spirit and purpose of his work, Judd claimed.

Second, " 'He is vulgar' " (iv). Judd did not regard the life of the common folk in New England or the realistic relating of that life to be vulgar. Judd admitted that he was thinking of the term in the least pejorative sense. Obed, for instance, was unrefined, rude, and simple, but not vulgar. It might be noted that Judd did not mention Pluck or Brown Moll.

Third, " 'He is unequal, grotesque, mermaiden, abrupt' " (iv). Here again, Judd said, was the question of what characterized the vulgar, the unrefined, and the ignoble. "May not rough rocks have a place in the fairest landscapes of nature or art?" (iv) he asked. "Have we not seen or heard of a cascade that starts, say, from the blue of the skies, pours down a precipe of rusty rock, and terminates in drift-wood and bog. Is that water *bathetic?* " (iv).

And, last, " 'He is no artist' " (iv). Perhaps not, Judd admitted, but he asked, "May there not be a moral as well as a material plot—a plot of ideas as well as incidents? 'Margaret' is a tale not of outward movement but of internal development. An obvious part of its plan is the three epochs of the life of its principal personage" (v). Referring to Master Elliman, Judd noted that he had been called a diluted imitation of Dominie Sampson. Judd's defense was that "the plot of the book involved this—that while Margaret grew up in, or contiguous to, a religious and civilized community, she should remain for the most part unaffected by these influences; yet she should not mature in ignorance, but should receive quite an amount of a species of erudition. To this effect the Master is introduced" (v). Judd admitted that the management of the role assigned to the Master was one of his most difficult tasks. Judd asserted that his purpose was never whimsical or consciously capricious; always he wished to be the artist.

VII   *The Revision (1851)*

Judd maintained that, in the revised version, sentences, not sentiments, had been changed, that words, not things, had been deleted. But a careful comparison of the first edition with the second will show that what Judd really did was to cut out, in the main, many of those passages which gave rise to the charge of vulgarity.

A few examples will suffice to indicate how Judd toned down his narrative. For instance, at the end of Chapter 5 of the first edition (1845), Margaret arrived at home with the rum that she had given up her spelling book to secure. The following is omitted in the revised edition:

"Is she come?" cried the father, waking from his sleep. "Give us a nip."

"None of your sneaking here, old bruiser!" broke out the mother, rising in bed. "You are a real coon that would suck the biggest cock dry."

They both drank, and Margaret, having eaten a morsel Chilion kept for her, went to bed. She had not been long asleep, when she was awakened by a noise below. Her father was calling her name, "Molly! Molly!" She started immediately to go down.

"Never mind, Margery," spoke Chilion, from his own chamber, as she descended the ladder. "He will come out of it soon."

Her father, overcome by his liquor, had fallen into a sort of delirium. "Bite, will ye? spit fire, ram lightning down a babe's throat, Molly! Molly!" She seized the convulsed arm of the old man, and rubbed it. "There, there," she said, "it will be over soon." Her mother lay trussed and frozen in sleep.

"Sweet angel," said the father; "hold on, put their tails in the stocks and let them squirm—Ha! ha! ha!" he laughed out, changing his tone. "There's pitch-forks, and swinging stands, and two Bibles dancing a hornpipe, and Deacon Penrose playing on a rum-hogshead."

"I shwum," cried Hash, swagging down the ladder, "if that an't a toping the whole. "Why didn't you tell me you had got back, Pegg?" He took the keg to make sure of what remained.

"Hash! Hash!" cried Margaret, "he thinks he's falling off the bridge, I can't hold him."

"Let him fall and be —— and you too," was the reply. The paroxysm began to subside, the old man's arm relaxed, his breathing became easier. Margaret reascended the stairs, whither Hash had already preceded her, and returned to that forgetfulness of all things which God vouchsafes even to the most miserable.[40]

Judd also deleted several passages in the revised edition having to do with the antics of the scoffers at the revival meetings. Nimrod, half-drunk, showed up, on one occasion, at a meeting and encouraged Bull to bite the mourners. The preacher declared Satan to be among them:

"I've cotched him by the tail," said another of the fry, twitching the dog, who thereupon renewed his roar.

"Pray, brethren, pray!" said the Preacher, and the people began to pray more lustily. "As with the sound of rams' horns the walls of Jericho fell down, so shall these sinners tremble before God."

"Where's Sibyl Radney?" cried one of the opposers. "She's got the bellows pipe for ye, and will let ye have some of the broomstick too, if you want."[41]

Later, Judd omitted another exchange between the preacher and Nimrod when he got around to "cleaning up" his novel.

Preacher. " . . . And here I espy the arch-adversary of souls, the contriver of your eternal ruin, the very devil himself in your midst."
Nimrod. "The devil you do."
Preacher. "Young man, you will have your portion in hell-fire."
Nimrod. "I go to hell if I do."
Preacher. "The deep damnation of God is prepared for you."
Nimrod. "I be damned if it is."[42]

Some of the more suggestive dialogue between the Widow and the Master concerning the value of her medicine for the treatment of the humors in women and some of the more rollicking songs in the "Husking Bee" chapter were omitted, as was the graphic description of the hanging of Chilion. In fact, in the revised edition, the description is not omitted, but blacked out. At the end of the chapter entitled "Margaret and Chilion," Judd appended a note, stating: "We have been chided for carrying the story of Chilion to so sad a termination. 'Shocking!' is the epithet applied to such management and such results. There is an illusion here. Nine-tenths of executions are equally shocking. The mistake is this: our readers look at Chilion from the Margaret side, and his home side, and his heart's side; as if every man that is hung had not a Margaret side, a home side, and his own heart side! . . . There would be no hangings if suspected individuals were to be regarded in the light in which some tender-hearted persons have allowed themselves to regard Chilion" (307).

VIII   *Compositions in Outline . . . from Judd's Margaret (1856)*

Sometime after the publication of the revised edition, Judd was flattered to receive from Felix O. C. Darley a letter asking permission to do a volume of illustrations depicting scenes from *Margaret*. Darley had already published illustrated volumes of Irving's *The Sketch Book* (1849), Frances Sargent Osgood's *Poems* (1850), John W. DeForest's *The History of the Indians of Connecticut (ca.* 1850), and Brackenridge's *Modern Chivalry* (1850). Darley's letter to Judd is lost, but obviously he told Judd of his determination to illustrate many of the great pieces of literature. Judd's reply has been preserved.

Augusta, Me, Dec. 31, 1851.

Dear Sir,

I know not that my Publishers will object to your request, and I am sure I do not, and therefore freely authorize you to use my Margaret for the purpose of your illustrations.

You will take the revised edition, in two vols. by Phillips & Sampson, Boston.

Wishing you success and peace in your great artistic mission (a great and good one it is in our world—) I am

Yours very truly
Sylvester Judd.[43]

Perhaps Judd's stipulation to Darley that he use the second edition was to preclude the depicting of any of the "vulgar" scenes Judd cut or the using of some of the "crude" dialogue of the first edition with the illustrations. Judd did not live to see Darley's *Compositions in Outline . . . from Judd's Margaret*, which was published in 1856. Had he lived he might have felt somewhat vindicated; if *Margaret* could inspire art, surely there must be something of art about it. There was, of course, in many of the scenes depicting the customs, conventions, lore, and language of another age and in many of the passages describing the landscape and natural phenomena. What Judd lacked was a narrative skill commensurate with his other talents and the ability to bury the preacher and the reformer in the artist.

CHAPTER 4

Philo: An Evangeliad *(1850)*

I *The Advent: The Christian Hope*

S HORTLY after the publication of *Margaret,* a lady to whom
the Reverend Edward Everett Hale had revealed the secret
of its authorship wrote Judd: "Have you a 'Mons Christi' where
you reside? Are you a happy household, living in peace and
comfort, where there are 'no wars, or rumors of wars'? — *I* should
like to become one of your company, if I shall not be compelled
to *leave my husband."*[1] Judd must have been pleased, as well as
amused, to receive such a letter — pleased that Mons Christi, "a
place not before described," should prove to be so appealing.
But Mons Christi, in Judd's view, was only the blueprint for *an*
ideal Christian community, a Christian consummation in a
localized setting, or what Sacvan Bercovitch has referred to as
Judd's Theopolis Americana.[2] Judd wanted the whole world to be
one grand Theopolis. Thus, he preached upon, meditated on, and
prayed for the coming of the Millennial Age. This was the
Christian hope, Judd confessed to a friend, that provided the
thread on which he strung the various scenes of *Philo.*

In Christian thought the idea of the Millennium has always
been associated with the Advent or the second coming of Christ.
In a letter to his friend Hale, written early in 1850, Judd
admitted that his interest in the subject went back some years
and that his initial interest was the result of the claims and
predictions of the Millerites,[3] an interest that sent him back to
the New Testament to see for himself what the biblical claims
were. Judd concluded "that Christ would come into the world
again, that he expected to come, and promised to come. But
how? *In the person of his followers:* in their virtues his would be

produced, in their moral beauty his would be pronounced; they would walk in his steps, bear his cross, die his death, illustrate his life, and so personate him. The *coming* of Christ, and his *revelations*, are terms used interchangeably by the evangelists, and by the Savior himself."[4]

The Advent, Judd pointed out, was always described in poetic terms. In fact, Judd said in his letter to Hale:

"He shall come with clouds and great glory." Here commences the Orientalism, or, as we should now say, the poetry of the thing. "The trump shall sound," — a poetical allusion to the jubilee fanfare of the Jews. "The dead shall be raised; even now," adds Christ, while he was then speaking, "they shall come forth from their graves"; the dead in sin, the carnally deceased. The theme is taken up by Paul, who expressly says, "Christ is *revealed in us*"; Peter energetically echoes the same idea, and speaks of the new heaven and new earth, *wherein dwellest righteousness;* and John in Patmos, finally throws the whole into a sublime poem, prophesy, or what you will.[5]

II   *In Defense of Dramatic Poesy*

In his review of Jones Very's *Essays and Poems* (1839), written in his senior year in divinity school, Judd said that "all things that constitute proper subjects for poetry demand to be re-viewed. They must be looked at with the soul. The vision of external things which have so long floated before the eyes of poets are something more than visions. They are charged with unperceived meaning; they have relations to the spirit, which the spirit alone can comprehend and interpret."[6] And what might be said of "the vision of external things" as a subject for poetic treatment could, Judd concluded in defense of the medium he chose for *Philo,* all the more be said when the vision was of heavenly things. The interpretation of prophesy was undeniably a task for the poet; it was one subject that must be approached through the soul. As Judd put it in a December 21, 1849, letter to Hale, "It is conceived that prophecy, the Apocalypse for example, was once poetry; and moreover that we shall fail to understand prophecy, until it is recast in its original form." Judd then added, "This observation applies particularly to that most interesting, yet most enigmatical matter, the second coming of Christ, &c. &c."[7]

Judd declared his poem to be "an epical or heroic attempt,"[8] a treatment of elevated Christian topics in blank verse. *Philo,* however, is dramatic in form. Judd may have shared the views of his friend Jones Very as expressed in Very's essay on "Epic Poetry," the first essay in *Essays and Poems,* where Very argued that the modern poet could not express the true heroic spirit since he, unlike Homer and Virgil, did not have "a region of fiction beyond history"[9] where he might set his action. Thus, if peculiarities of the epic are no longer possible, the modern poet must turn to the *dramatic* as the only viable substitute for evoking the moods and feelings associated with the epic. The Christian dramatic poet, Very argued, is fortunate in that he can, like the epic poet, reveal "to his age forms of nobler beauty and heroism than dwells in the minds of those around him."[10] To him is available the epic technique of giving the gods visible appearances; and, thereby, he can throw over "his whole subject a sublimnity which it could not otherwise have had, giving occasion to nobler description, and tending to excite that admiration which is the leading aim of the epic."[11] However, to "surround his heroes with supernatural agents, capable of raising for his action the highest admiration,"[12] is no easy task. Yet, Very contended, Dante's *Divine Comedy* plainly shows that the tendency that Christianity gave to poetry was not to the epic but to the dramatic. Judd's *Philo* is an "attempt" after the manner advocated by Very.

According to Arethusa Hall, Judd began the composition of *Philo* late in 1845 and completed it early in 1848. The *Literary World* for November 17, 1849, listed *Philo* for "immediate publication." The book, published by Phillips, Sampson and Co. and bearing the date 1850, was deposited for copyright on December 28, 1849. The 244-page poetic drama was issued in two bindings—one of black cloth stamped in gold, the other of red cloth stamped in gold with gilt edges.

III   *The Poem*

A.   *Gabriel's Visit*

Philo is not divided into acts; for, as Milton said of his dramatic poem *Samson Agonistes,* it was not intended for the stage. Rather it is divided into twenty-one scenes, several of which are

set in the space above the earth or in the regions below or within
the earth. Scene one, the exposition and the longest of the poem,
introduces Philo, the ideal Christian, Charles, the scoffer, and
the heavenly visitor, the Archangel Gabriel. The scene ends with
a sorrowful lament over the evils of slavery, but with a prophecy
of its eventual abolition. Even before the scene opens, Gabriel
had arrived in Philo's village, having been sent there by Christ to
determine the truth of a report that had reached heaven that on
earth the church and the state had sold out to sin. Gabriel had
spent the night in the village, looking about, gazing into the
changeless sky, and reliving in memory the creation of the earth.
With the opening of the scene, Philo informed Charles that he
was looking for a stranger about whom he had had a vision in the
night. Gabriel appeared and announced that he had been sent to
find a certain Philo. Philo identified himself and expressed a
regret that he had not been permitted to be Gabriel's host for
the night. Gabriel then sounded the theme of the poem:

> *Gabriel.* I have no lack. Love is my food, my bed,
> And roof. Love is my wing, my impulse love,
> And soul and circumstance, my joy and prayer.
> In love I dwell in God, and God in me.
> Not otherwise is seen the great Unseen;
> And the high host of us, in love, all dwell
> Together, brother, sister, cherubim.
> Heaven, stars, time, place, and their inhabitants,
> Subsist in love—as love itself in God—
> Wherethrough these maples leaf, and those thick clouds
> Their lustre draw. In love are visitors,
> Attendance, ministry, and fellowship;
> Sphere answering to sphere, and heart to heart,
> Within the Soul of All, concentrical;
> To seraph, seraph speaking, musical
> And glad; inaudible to sin alone.
> Truly I nothing crave, but that you love,
> And mortals all; whence it shall come to pass,
> That our effulgent scope shall earth comprise,
> And, man into the flaming circle falling,
> This human state reflect the heavenly.[13]

Gabriel manifested interest in the various church buildings.
Philo, embarrassed to admit that so many different ones existed,
pointed to an arbor by the river where he and a band of kindred

spirits met to worship. Christ, Philo declared, was the preface to
his every interest. At this point, Gabriel began to reminisce about
his part and that of the other angels in announcing the birth of
Christ, reviewed the life and mission of Christ, and declared
Christ to be the fulfillment of prophecy. Then Gabriel asked
about Christ's church —

> That fraternity he formed
> Of godlike minds, and bodies luminous,
> Intemerate, holy natures, called the church; —
> How does it? (13)

Gabriel was pleased when Philo pointed to a group of children
at a rural festival because Christ

> . . . loved the dew
> Of childhood; fairest imagery of his
> Own innocence, ere dried by worldliness,
> Or shaken by a rude utility. (15)

The children were singing a hymn. Gabriel conducted a
catechism and, to his delight, found that the children in their
innocence loved everyone.

But at Gabriel's admission that he never was a child nor felt
the pangs of weak humanity, Philo seized the opportunity to ask
Gabriel about "Angelage."

> *Gabriel.* O'er will of mortals we do not preside;
> That is prerogative of God alone;
> Nor sermons preach, nor life lay down, like Christ.
> An influence we, like memory of youth,
> That combs in sea-like, on the reef of feeling,
> Charming the soul with an immortal hope.
> Anon, as midnight music, we arrest
> The ear of sin, and make the wanton pause;
> We writhle from the skies, in maple keys;
> The conscience hears our voice, in sister tones,
> And hatred melts into pure human love.
> We brood o'er steps of helpless orphanage,
> As sunbeams flicker on that slighted moss.
> All souls have guardians, that follow them,
> As hopes of fathers hover round their sons.
> Of nature's laws, by man so named, the gift

> Is not with us to bind or loose. But this,
> To-day, I have, in specialty from Christ,
> To be invisible or visible,
> And make you so, and traverse space and time. (22-23)

B. *"O, Lost, Lost, Lost America!"*

Gabriel and Philo set out in flight and were soon over the Carolinas. There on a river's brink they saw a naked black man with waled and bloody back. He was a runaway slave, but the hounds were near; and he had determined to take his own life rather than to endure more flogging and slavery. He had just time, before drowning himself, to tell Gabriel and Philo his story. While his master's daughter slept, he borrowed her books, taught himself to read, and developed an overwhelming desire for freedom. The slave and the lovely white girl became close friends, so much so that the young girl helped the slave escape. But after four days of freedom, he was caught and flogged. He fled again, determined this time never to be taken alive. Gabriel, in commenting on the slave's death, revealed to Philo that the time would come when the people would build a pyre of whips and fetters and all signs of slavery and that the time would come when the races would live as brothers.

In the second scene, entitled "Air and Earth," Judd got quickly to the culminating evil—war. Gabriel and Philo continued their flight, a panoramic one, ranging from pole to pole. But Philo was so disturbed by what he saw that he begged Gabriel to take him back "to my mother-land, most good,/Most bad America" (35). Their flight took them over the heights of Monterey, where the Mexican War was being fought. There, reminiscent of Milton's Death, was a shape "thrice more terrible than Death;/Hybrid of Sin and Hell" (37). Gabriel informed Philo that the shape was War. But War disclaimed any responsibility for what was going on. Philo lamented:

> O, lost, lost, lost America!
> O, utterly undone! damned, damned forever!
> Was wealth of worlds e'er cast so vile away!
> Thy government turns out a worthless sham.
> Thy history is black, as black as hell,
> Nor can it e'er be written clean. . . .
> . . . A war,
> A freeman's war in aid of slavery!
> Had ever strife so poor a countenance? (39-41)

Philo uttered a prayer that love would return and forestall the ruin of America.

C. *King Expediency*

Following an interlude that celebrated the selfless human love of Philo and Annie, a love that strengthened and beautified their lives, Gabriel brought Philo from his state of euphoria to one of sobering reality with a political allegory. The great King of the realm was named Expediency. A company of bishops, generals, politicians, and judges gathered about the King. A judge confessed that he hanged a young man because he wished to make him an example and a warning to others. The bishop admitted that, to protect his authority in all matters of divinity, he stamped even valid religious views "Infidelity" when such seemed expedient. The King approved of the action of the bishop, but became greatly disturbed by a general who developed a case of conscience.

> *The King.* Didst thou say "Conscience"?
> Methought the word escaped thee.
> *The General.*   I said it.
> *The King.* 'Tis slang, and most offensive to good taste.
> *The General.* Conscience it was, my life upon it, sharp—
> *The King.* Tut, tut! you make yourself ridiculous.
> *The General.* Conscience!
> *The King.* I beg of thee, my liege, don't speak so loud;
> You will be heard; our enemies will triumph,
> And our good cause be hagged with consciences.
> *The General.* Conscience!! (66)

The King ordered the general removed and his lips pressed. It was given to Charles, who witnessed the scene at court, to set forth the meaning of the allegory from the standpoint of expediency:

> 'Tis Policy that rules
> The whole. A soul is but an evil spirit,
> That doth the superstitious race annoy;
> . . . .
> . . . Expediency doth helm all movements
> All councils prompt; the pious conclave sway,
> And caucus. . . . (68-69)

D. *Faith, Hope, Love*

Judd set his next scene in the sacred groves. Philo and Annie went there to pray, but instead they were surprised by the discovery of a beautiful lady asleep on the leaves. Gabriel appeared, identified the lady as the Spirit of Love, and pointed to her two sisters—Faith and Hope—who rested nearby. Love, discouraged because the earth wanted none of her charms, had asked Gabriel to cast a spell on her that she might rest and forget. But Annie wanted to hear the voice of Love and to learn the mystery of Faith and Hope. Gabriel called upon the Spirit of Love to arise since a mortal love was now ready for her message. Love asked if the Mexican War had ended; it had not, she was told by Gabriel. Love wished then to be made oblivious again to the evils of the world, but Gabriel had determined that the three sisters would tell their story to the two lovers.

The history of the world since Christ walked the earth had been one of war, sectarian strife, and evils of all sorts. The cross Faith put in the churches had been trodden under foot in sectarian broils and iron creeds. The religious bodies feared to love each other. According to Love, the three sisters survived the Middle Ages by boarding with the Dryads. The promise of the Reformation soon vanished in the wake of religious wars and revolutions. The sisters set their hearts then on America; but even in America they found religious persecution, slaughter of the Indians, expediency, not justice, practiced in the land, and wars after wars. In America, Love wanted to unbind humanity by revealing the secrets of love; she wanted to convince John C. Calhoun and William Lloyd Garrison that they were one in soul. She wanted to melt the frozen nations on which now the Sun of Righteousness shone but cold and dull:

> I would join man and man, fold realm in realm,
> Reticulate the surface of the earth
> With chains of loving minds, all hand in hand;
> Give slips of heavenly bloom to every child,
> While Faith and Hope should teach the culturing;
> Sin-buried life exhume; with silver trump
> Should be announced the Resurrection morn;
> The disembodied Soul of Goodness find
> Its heaven here, new heaven promised long. (84)

E. The Devil and the Problem of Evil

From the sylvan groves Judd shifted his scene to hell. And at this point, Judd began his argument that was designed "to drive the theological devil from the world and from the universe." He would allow "no foreign, infernal, super-human agency" in the world.[14] Philo, seeing himself as a latter-day Dante, was taken on the tour by Gabriel for the purpose of providing Philo with an opportunity to interview the Devil. Philo in hell did not see the souls in torment that he expected to see, although it was apparent from the remarks of the Devil that hellfire did exist. An amusing dialogue ensued between the Devil and Philo:

> *The Devil.* Be just with me, 'tis all I ask.
> You tax on me all mischief of the earth;
> If preachers bastardize, the Devil did it;
> If converts fall from grace, the Devil did it;
> If men make rum, besure, the Devil does it;
> I'm somewhat dirty, that I own, but that's
> Because they throw a deal of dirt at me. (90–91)

Philo wanted to know if the Devil went about seeking whom he might devour, if he gilded lust and cheapened virtue, and if he formed covenants with sinners. And what about the stench Philo smelled? It was only, the Devil said, the odor of the mutilated bodies newly arrived from Vera Cruz, where "Christian" forces were locked in combat.

The Devil admitted that he was among the first to cry out, "Crucify him, crucify!" when Christ was being condemned; but when he heard Christ on the cross ask the Father to forgive them, he fell as one dead and has ever since been a wanderer upon the earth. "You are the Wandering Jew!" Philo said. "They call me Devil;/I know no other name" (93), the Devil replied. The Devil denied that he was at the bottom of the Salem witchcraft trials. In fact, his had been a hard lot: he was held responsible for adultery and murder, for illegitimacy, and for the carnage of war; yet, though he had no soul, he had a human shape and would harm no human soul. Men were responsible for their *own* evil.

Philo was confused. "Unriddle me, instructor mine, is there/No other Devil?" (96) Philo asked Gabriel. Gabriel declared that he

had never seen another. Who, then, Philo wanted to know,
tempted the Son of God? He was, Gabriel said, tempted by pride
and avarice, as are all men; but he put them behind him. Did not
the angels rebel against the Almighty, Philo asked, and, thereby,
fall? "Could Faith, or Hope, or Love abandon God?" (97)
Gabriel replied. *No* infernal, superhuman force or being
operated in the affairs of men, Philo was informed.

The next scene, set in "Philo's Garden," is a debate between
Charles and Philo. Charles maintained that God had forgotten
his creation and that the Bible was even being used to support
slavery and war—arguments that troubled Philo deeply. Philo
fleed to "An Arbor," where he prayed,

> Father in Heaven, my Father, and my God,
> Resolve me,—Why is Evil? Whence, and Whither?
> This mystery unloose, this weary sum
> Explain. (113)

The Voice of the Wisdom of God came to Philo and reminded
him that frail humanity could not understand all of the mysteries
of God. Man's duty was to trust God. In God's wisdom man was
given freedom of the will; and when he exercises that freedom
and sins, sin punishes itself; and man falls into the pit he himself
has dug. But recovery is found in the gospel of Christ. Using an
argument closely akin to Emerson's notion of the privative
nature of evil, the Voice of the Wisdom of God declared:

> The Evil dies when Good revives; it is
> Probational, and ends when this begins.
> Evil is the exception, not the rule;
> 'Tis incidental, not habitual.
> Crimes remedy themselves or overthrow,
> Calamity confirms the strength of hope;
> Weakness is quality of finite things,
> And marks the progress to Infinity. (115)

Man, Philo was reminded, is God's last and noblest work,
responsible for his own actions, but

> The final or the primal cause of sin
> Tis not for men to know, theirs to amend.
> God keeps his secrets to himself. (118)

F. *The Call for Reform*

There follows in "Philo's Rooms" a discussion concerning the characteristics of the ideal pastor, poet, and lawyer. The pastor said that Christ's minister is possessed of Christ, subscribes to no creed, allows nothing to come between him and God, reviews all man-made laws in the light of the Gospel, and attacks with words public vice. He is, in reality, a reformer, pledged to peace, freedom, temperance, and unity. His office demands that he provide spiritual instruction for his age. The poet described the ideal poet as one whose inward self bears a resemblance to that of all men. His motivation is a deep love for mankind. Love irrigates his soul, and he lives neighborlike to heaven, reporting "Divinity in its selectest modes" (127). The ideal lawyer must be a statesman who defends the land, promotes trade, encourages the arts of peace, and extends democracy. The Christian statesman recognizes God's government as supreme and absolute in the land and lays no stress in jails, but on reform. Judd for himself, in the person of the pastor, declared:

> That all should be Reformers is my thought;
> The Clergy, Statesmen, Poets, every guild,
> Estate, profession, calling. The Reformer
> Is inorganic in society,
> No wheel in the machinery of life;
> But needful as Physicians are, to cure
> Diseases of the time. (133)

One of the most amusing scenes is entitled "A Steamboat." The steamboat was both a microcosm of society and a symbol of man's technological progress. The personified abstractions—Love, Faith, and Hope—were aboard, as were the pastor, Charles, Annie, and Philo. Charles had, in addition, invited his friend the Devil along in order, he said, to convert him. Although the Devil had no soul and could not experience a spiritual conversion, he could, once he was no longer held responsible for the sins of the world, become an effective reformer; for he had, as he informed his enthralled listeners on board the steamboat, lived in every eye and kernel of evil.

> *The Devil.* I've muckered around in lanes,
> Ditches, and garrets, hovels, hospitals.
> I am excited; I go for reform.

. . . .
. . . I go down with all,
Down to the bottom, grub among the settlings,
For that has been my avocation; wherefore
I can tell ye, there is no music there,
Nor dancing; maidens never smile, but glout,
And stare at you like stupid walruses.
I wish I was a man like ye, I do,
Or had a tongue like one whom I heard speak.
But I've no soul; yet in my kidneys, friends,
I feel these things are horrible; and how
Men with souls can be calm, in such a pass,
Is what amazes me. (166–67)

In what is perhaps the most truly poetic scene in the entire
poem, Philo related to Annie the story of an encounter he had
with the Genius of America, whose text was Repent and whose
theme was the Advent. America must prepare the way of the
Lord; but, like Rome, America must be humbled; America must
mend her ways:

Think upon your ways, reform
Your doings. Give the Indians homes, enfeoff
Those nomades; free your slaves; unhand the soil.
Repent and shun dismantlement of doom;
Few years have done for you the work of ages,
By forelock ye have ta'en degeneracy,
And copied ills ye had not time to grow. (195)

Ministers must cease to water down eternal truth for the sake of
expediency. The nation must disband the military and spend the
wasted revenues on schools, parks, and the arts.

G. "Every Knee Shall Bow and Every Tongue Confess"

In the next to the last scene, Gabriel declared his work to be at
an end, but just what work Gabriel has in mind the reader is not
quite sure. Early in the poem, Gabriel said his mission was to seek
out the truth of some matters relative to the church and the
state. Now he seems to be the harbinger of the Advent. King
Expediency, Gabriel announces, is set for a hard fight in
Armageddon. An earthquake will burst the chains of slavery and
shake down the prison walls of injustice and cause men to know
that God is sovereign. Christ is to be revealed, and all kindred,

tribes, and tongues are to be gathered unto him. Philo declares that the dragons of War, Slavery, and Intemperance, along with the Evils of Bigotry, Monopoly, and Oppression, will be bound in chains to await the Judgment.

It is given to Philo to announce the actual culminating event:

> *Philo.* Lo, He comes! our Lord
> And Christ; he comes to judge the world; or, more
> To let his truth exert judicial force,
> Dividing soul and spirit, joint and marrow.
> The halo crowns his uncrowned head; a Name
> Is written on his vesture and his thigh:
> THE LORD OF LORDS AND KING OF KINGS. (224-25)

The Innocent Distresses—such as Poverty and Ignorance—fell down at Christ's feet and wept. He invited empires and men who felt his design to obey the instincts of the hour. Too long they had not heeded the voice of Conscience, had not visited the prisoners, had not healed the sick. They had given lip service to him as Guide and Head, but had gone about killing and cursing their enemies and fighting wars. While he delayed his coming, they gave support to sin. Christ said:

> God lays no measures hard,
> Or hard to be discerned. He loveth you;
> Ye were dear sons and pleasant children all,
> And he would dwell with you, walk in your midst.
> And me, his Son, your Way, and Truth, and Life,
> He gave; nor lacked there ought for your perfection.
> I came to save, and still to save am come.
> I will not heap reproach, nor need I add
> To what your quickened apprehensions feel.
> Is this your sin well charged?
> *The People.* The awful guilt
> O Lord, we own.
> *Christ.* Shall't be destroyed?
> *The People.* Amen,
> So let it be; the execution haste. (229)

Then the Phantasms of the Evil call for the rocks to hide them. The Kings of the Earth confess their sinfulness and cast their crowns before Christ and return their governments to him. The Politicians confess to the infamy of thwarting Christ's redemp-

tive plan. Bishops and Clergymen confess that they controlled
the people by catering to their passions, bowing before the
statues of men, not before the statutes of God. Even the Pope of
Rome confesses to thrusting a carnal government between the
Church and Christ.

The Transcendentalists too are brought to confession, admitting there that Christ was the greatest miracle of all times and
that he came to bring the Eternal Word, but that they had
chosen to find truth within themselves.

The Transcendentalists. In homage, due to goodness, Lord, we bend
To thee, who Goodness art. O Wonderful
Of the create, O Miracle of time!
Thou curdled breath of rare divinity,
Thou soul of Virtue, globed in human eyes,
Eternal Word on ruddy lips incarne!
Too oft on self we gazed, and less on thee:
To-day the mirror's broken; let it lie,
Since God through thee and us is shining fair.
. . . .
Our fount ran dry, alas! good Lord; and now
We bring our empty bowls to thee. We shone,
But inward, oven-suns, none blessed our light;
Lord, bless us; we will bless, unsought, unspent. (232)

Christ ordered from his sight all adulteries, unnatural affections, heresies, wrath, murder, unbelief, idolatries, abominations,
and whatever defiles; they were to be consumed with
unquenchable flame. Christ himself flowed into humanity and
was acknowledged on all lips. Even the Wandering Jew, no
longer called the Devil, declared that

                    In sulphur flames,
          War crisps and shudders like a burning feather.
          Intemperance with all her crew is drowned
          And dissipated in that lake of fire.
          Fast to a stake with her own manacles,
          The fagots blaze about the Dragoness,
          Fell Slavery; a hissing tempest beats
          Oppression down; the carcasses of Lust
          And Avarice are broiling; Slander gnaws
          Her tongue; Deceits like adders wimble through
          The singeing vapors, and expires; Force falls

> And Hate in the conflagrant vengeance.—Lo!
> The fires go out; the Sun, all genially,
> Shines on the ruin. (238)

And Philo informs Annie that the noise she hears is swords being beaten into plowshares, slaves frolicking, freemen at work, and jails being converted into hospitals. As the Millennial rapture spreads abroad, Philo envisions a Constitutional Convention to Christianize the Constitution as America becomes truly Theopolis Americana.

IV *The Way of Critics*

Within days of its publication, Judd shipped off a copy of *Philo* to Edward Everett Hale, stating, "What may be the fortune of 'Philo,' I am neither prophet nor poet enough to tell."[15] Hale's comments on the poem must have been cautious or evasive, for Judd, in his letter of January 11, 1850, sensing the worst, wrote to Hale that "what is a luminous road to me may be a heap of odious stumbling-blocks to some others."[16] Even to such a sympathetic friend, Judd then felt it incumbent to explain what he intended in *Philo,* a fact boding ill for the poem:

[*Philo*] admits of (poetical) supernatural agencies in Gabriel, &c It looks, from the Christian or Christ's point of view, at men and things in the world. The fancy of "the devil" is designed to drive the theological devil from the world and from the universe. . . . It teaches, moreover, that the hope of the world lies in itself; in its men and women, its wood and iron, and in the blessed gospel of the Son of God, which also it has. It alludes to the evils, and more particularly to that culminating one, war. In Charles is expressed the sceptical, profane, dark side of things, &c. &c. It winds up with a poetical account of that which I believe to be the consummation of the wish, purpose, and plan of Jesus,—the Advent; that which Christ most literally, truthfully, and earnestly conceived; which was to his eye the grandest of all visions, and which he—and how could he do otherwise?—spoke of in terms borrowed from the imagination; borrowed, too, from the imagination of the sacred books of his people; borrowed from, and belonging to, the imagination of all times.
Is this apparent, or is it closed to the common reader of the book?[17]

If Hale replied to the query, his reply has not been located. In

fact, Hale may not have wanted to tell Judd what should have
been as obvious to Judd as it must have been to the common
reader: Judd lost control of his material. The poem lacks unity
because the thread Judd thought he had used to string his
episodes together is not evident in most of the episodes—
episodes that range from the utterly serious to the slightly
ludicrous. In essence, what Judd does is to give the reader a
compendium of the sins and evils of the world along with an
inconclusive theological discussion of the nature of evil and a
rather amusing account of the transformation of the theological
Devil into the Wandering Jew, who becomes, then, one of the
"good ole boys." Even the heavenly visitors seem no more than
helpless observers of the earthly scene. With Love, Faith, and
Hope loose in the world, there was, even so, little evidence that
the love of Christ was taking up its abode in a significant number
of hearts. Perhaps in all honesty, Judd himself saw no evidence in
his day that America or the nations of the earth were becoming
more Christ-like. And yet in Judd's view the Millennium would
not come as a cataclysmic event as depicted by the biblical
writers; it would come quietly and progressively as Christ set up
his reign in the hearts of men, a prophetic truth that Judd was
convinced of. But when, five-sixths of the way through the poem,
Judd has Gabriel announce that his work is finished, the world is
no more prepared for Christ's Advent than when the poem
opened. Judd had not developed his theme. Perhaps he could not
figure out how to bring it off. Thus, at the Advent, knees had to
bow; confession had to be made; and *only then* were the evils of
the world destroyed in one grand climactic event and the reign
of Christ instituted.

As usual, Judd was sensitive to the reaction of his contempo-
raries, many of whom apparently regarded *Philo* as some sort of
unfortunate joke. Why Judd in late March 1850 wrote the
Reverend Henry W. Bellows, New York clergyman and coeditor
with Samuel Osgood of the *Christian Inquirer,* is not clear unless
Judd was hoping to forestall some more unfavorable and, in
Judd's view, unwarranted criticism in the event *Philo* was
reviewed in Bellows's journal. The letter may be, however, only
an answer to an inquiry from Bellows or a response to a request
for a copy of *Philo.* No matter what prompted it, the letter is a
plaintive plea from a troubled author for critical fairness.

Augusta, March 24, 1850.

Bro. Bellows,

Allow me a few words, in all friendliness and good feeling, touching the book "Philo," and things pertinent thereto.

The book has been received with great levity in some quarters, and, if I may so say, *immorally* received in others.

Is there no such thing as the Morality of Criticism? Do not the canons of literary judgment imply at least *candor* ? Have Authors no rights? Is an Author entitled to less respect than a tin-pedler? Are his wares thrown beyond the pale of ordinary consideration?

For instance, the Literary World taxes "Philo" with "undisguised Infidelity." This is rather a grave charge whether against a man, an opinion, or a book; against that withal which professes to be, and labors to be, full of Christianity.

You say, O, that is the way of Critics. Is it a good way, is it an honorable way, is it a way that would be tolerated in any other relation of civilized society?

"Philo" is, at least, a serious book, wrought out in uttermost seriousness of spirit, its apparent humor or recklessness is wrung from the bitterness, of the heart.

Of course it comes within the purlieu of criticism; but I ask, has criticism no Morality?

It is a book, or is designed to be, of Christian ideas. Christian? Not nominal Christian; but Christ's own ideas. It applies the Christian, Christ's own idea, to life, Society, government, the world, nature, &c; even unto the glorious consummation which Christ himself predicted, of his Second Coming.

That Second Coming, so gorgeously, so pathetically expressed by Jesus, what does it mean, I have thought much about it,—moved perhaps thereto by Father Miller, and have sought, poetically, to set it forth. The anticipation of such an event, fulfilment, runs all through the book. I have felt moreover that Prophecy, sacred, evangelical, veritable Prophecy, would never be understood by us, by people generally, till it was translated into Poetry, or rather, till it was reproduced in its original form, which was the Poetical. Hence, Philo.

Christ comes when his spirit fills hearts, when love reigns, when truth and virtue abound, does he not? He comes in us, from our faces flashes the light that darts as the lightning from one side of the heavens to the other, is it not so?

Well, Philo, in looking over the earth, goes into its depths and centre. Why, to see what elements of hope, of a Christian and human hope are there. He is present at a death scene, to see how a Christian can die. He loves a woman, because that love consists with, and blends in with, our highest ideal of the Christian, and of a true, character. &c, &c.

I have felt, moreover, that Calvinism has its "Course of Time." Is there nothing for Unitarians? for a rational and liberal Christianity, that is, for Christianity itself?

But, did it become to ask myself the question, "Who am I, that I should go unto Pharaoh?"

But, as you see, I undertook to go. I have wished that Christianity, Christianity that is above sect or creed, Christ's Christianity might be furthered among men. For this I preach, and pray, and that book is part of my preaching and praying; therefore I say it is a serious book.

Please accept the book, which ought to have gone to you before; and excuse what I have written, if it needs excuse, and believe me

very truly yours,
Sylvester Judd.

N.B.   I do not seek to extenuate the faults of "Philo," but simply to vindicate its purpose.[18]

Unlike the publication of *Margaret*, the publication of *Philo* went largely unnoticed by the leading journals of the day. Only the *North American Review* for April 1850 gave it a full critical treatment, and that was of the sort Judd deplored in his letter to Henry Bellows. The reviewer, Andrew Preston Peabody—pastor over the South Parish Unitarian Church in Portsmouth, New Hampshire, author of *Lectures on Christian Doctrine* (1844), and later Plummer Professor of Christian Morals and Ethics at Harvard—admitted that he knew Judd personally and considered him a friend. But that did not cause Peabody to temper his remarks. "The most glaring fault of the author of Margaret and Philo," he wrote, "is that he personates alternately the copyist and the poet. He vaults from the kitchen to the clouds, and leaps from the clouds into the gutter; he paints an angel's face over the tavern-bar, and thrusts a Dominie Sampson into the councils of Olympus."[19] Peabody acknowledged, however, that *Philo* was an original work, even if some of its general features were suggested by other books, such as Bailey's *Festus*, a dramatic poem that also pictured a mingling of Archangels and mortals in heaven, on the earth, and elsewhere. But again Judd found himself accused of something approaching vulgarity. Peabody wrote: "He is too familiar with the best literature of all times, not to have the canons of good taste at his easy command. He need not fear their constraint. They cannot cripple his freedom. He is too strong to be their slave. But if he will make himself their master, there are no laurels too high for his reach."[20] Judd surely regarded the review as damning, despite the faint praise.

CHAPTER 5

Richard Edney and the Governor's Family *(1850)*

I *The Garden Theory of the Tale*

JUDD wrote most of *Richard Edney and the Governor's Family. A Rus-Urban Tale, Simple and Popular, Yet Cultured and Noble, Of Morals, Sentiment, and Life, Practically Treated and Pleasantly Illustrated containing, also, Hints on Being Good and Doing Good* in the interval between the completion of *Philo* and its publication in 1850. Its purpose, Judd said, was to indicate "what was expected of a man,"[1] and to show what a man can make of himself by the exercise of his own inherent spiritual powers. Judd set his tale in Woodylin, a thinly veiled representation of Augusta; and individual families—including that of his father-in-law—and other persons drawn from life, including himself, people his *roman à clef.*

Judd realized that his novel of sensibility was a hodgepodge of styles, modes, digressions, political allegory, social criticism, hermeneutics, and literary borrowings, so much so that, in the middle of his novel, he devoted much of a chapter—one of several lengthy digressions in the tale—to a fanciful defense of what he had done. He wrote:

A Tale may be like a garden, one quarter of which shall be devoted to cereal grain, another to kitchen sauce, a third shall be reserved for fruits, while the fourth is gay with flowers, and the connection between the parts consists of naked paths alone; yet it is a garden,—. . . . So a Tale may have its various departments, the only apparent connection between which shall be the leaves of the book and enumeration of the

106

chapters, and still please Historical taste. There is a real connection in both instances;—in the first, it is that of the brooding and immanent power of Nature, which is always a unity and a beauty; in the last, it is the heart of the Author, which is likewise a unity, and should be a beauty.

A Tale is like this June morning, when I am now writing. I hear from my open windows the singing of birds, the rumble of a stage-coach, and the blacksmith's anvil. . . . Over all, hangs the sun; down upon the village looks that eye of infinite blessedness, and into the scene that urn of exhaustless beauty pours beauty. . . . This morning's sun idealizes everything. Nature is not shocked at toads. A Tale might be thus diversified; and if through it streamed love and gladness from the soul of the writer, like sunlight, the structure would still be harmonious, and the effect pleasing.

A Tale is like human life,—of which, indeed, it purports to be a transcript,—and human life exhibits some contrast. . . . Through all the peace and delight of one's being will be heard the perpetual wail of some sad memory, even as I now hear, in this sunny morning, the melancholy note of the peewee. (307–309)

A modern reader may not be willing to accept Judd's cavalier—or perhaps tongue-in-cheek—defense of his discursive tale, nor is he likely to find the unity in the novel Judd asserted was there. In fact, the plot of the novel—the type of story made popular some years later by another Unitarian minister, Horatio Alger, Jr.—seems, at times, little more than a convenient vehicle Judd employed to sound anew the social, religious, and political themes that the minister and reformer in him demanded that he sound.

II   *The Tale*

A. *Poor Richard*

The tale opens with the hero, Richard—a name obviously borrowed from Benjamin Franklin—trudging his way through a snowstorm toward the city of Woodylin. Richard was young; Richard was happy; and "he rejoiced in the feeling of these herald drops on his cheeks" ([7]). A deeply religious lad, Richard knew that the Almighty had said to the snow, " 'Be thou on the earth'; and he felt that the Divine Providence cared for the lilies of the field as well in their decay as in their bloom; and

that a ceaseless Benignity was covering the beds where they lay
with the lovely raiment of the seasons, and cherishing in the cold
ground the juices that should, after a brief interval, spring forth
again, and create a gladsome resurrection of nature" (9).

With a secure faith, Richard was coming to the city to earn
money to help his father pay off a mortgage on the farm; but
more than anything else, he wanted "to glorify God and benefit
man; yet was he ignorant, practically ignorant of the many arts
by which selfishness, vanity, and false systems of society,
disintegrate character, and undermine virtue" (81). The tale,
then, is about Richard's attempt to remain virtuous as he
struggled against people and temptations such as he had not
encountered before. He planned to live in the city with his sister
Roxy, her husband, Asa Munk, and the couple's two little girls,
Memmy and Bebby.

B. *The Governor's Family*

Soon after his arrival in Woodylin, Richard became acquainted
with some of the daughters of Governor Dennington—Barbara,
Eunice, Melicent, and Rowena. Richard was especially attracted
to Barbara and Melicent, both of whom were Christians; but the
two approached their religion differently and sought to express
their Christian concerns in different ways. "Barbara aspired
after, and sometimes stumbled in pursuit of, the infinities of the
universe,—Melicent delighted to yield herself to the serene,
unconscious currents of immortal life. . . . Barbara had more
ideality,—Melicent more purity. . . . In respect of humanity,
Barbara was an abolitionist,—Melicent gave herself to the cause
of Peace. Barbara had great hope for the race,—Melicent a
strong faith in it" (35). It is easy to guess which of the young
ladies most appealed to Judd and thus to Richard, who, in many
respects, resembled the poor boy Judd, who would marry into a
wealthy political family. Judd's own story might well have been
entitled *Sylvester and the Senator's Family*.

In fact, the Governor's family, to whom Chapter 2 is devoted,
is likely modeled after the family of Senator Reuel Williams.
Governor Dennington is probably an idealized portrait of
Senator Williams; and his daughters Jane Elizabeth, whom Judd
married, and Zilpha, her younger sister, may have sat for the
portraits of Melicent and Barbara. Jane was slender, delicate, and
very feminine; politically she was a radical Democrat and

philosophically "something of a Transcendentalist"[2]—or so she was when Judd first met her. Zilpha was more extroverted than Jane, but both were good Unitarians. Little biographical information is available about Senator Williams's wife, Sarah, except that she was an Episcopalian rather than a Unitarian;[3] and to identify her with Madame Dennington would have to be a little more tenuous than in the case of the other members of the Williams family.

The Williams family was famous for its hospitality. The family guest book carried the signatures of President James K. Polk, Secretary of the Navy George Bancroft, President Josiah Quincy of Harvard, and John Lothrop Motley, the historian, as well as those of other prominent people. The Williams's mansion—one of Maine's most notable dwellings—sat on a high ridge overlooking the town of Augusta. It was carpeted with an imported Brussels carpet; an oil painting by Gilbert Stuart hung on the wall; mirrors from England, a highboy from Japan, a mahogany wine cooler, silver bowls, and other evidences of affluence graced the mansion. Judd wrote *Richard* in his own house next door.

C. *A Worthy American Family: A Portrait*

To picture an admirable American family—regardless of how closely (or remotely) it might have resembled the family into which Judd married—was one of Judd's purposes in the novel. As he said in Chapter 2, "We offer this chapter to our readers, not because it contains matters rare or striking;—it does not; it is of common and familiar things;—and because it is of common and familiar things, we write it. It is a simple picture of a worthy American family, that we would like to preserve, but which we are anxious to present to our distant readers" (36).

Judd indicated that by distant readers he meant the English, French, German, Swedish, and others. Then in an almost nonsensical flight of fancy, Judd said that "if license can be had from the Imperial Commission of Turkey, and our friend, Ees Hawk Effendi, of Constantinople, amidst other engagements, shall be able to complete the translation, we hope to publish the book in that celebrated metropolis" (37). Continuing, Judd argued that, since the Anglo-Saxons and Normans came primarily from the banks of the Caspian, it naturally follows that soi-disant Americans trace their ancestry to the land of Genghis Khan and

Tamerlane. "Consider then," Judd said, "the pleasure of
introducing a work like this among our almost forgotten
ancestors" (37). But, alas, he foresaw problems when the work
was introduced to "our Usbek relatives and Ottoman friends,"
who "will not understand the term, 'American family.' They will
naturally associate the Governor, his kindred and contempo-
raries, with the Russians of Alaska" (38). Judd asked himself the
question, "Why not call them a New England family?" He
answered, "For the reason that they are not; but a United States
of North American one" (38). He concluded: "And certainly, if
this volume is to go among the Tartars, we cannot but be anxious
that the introduction be as smooth and unencumbered as
possible" (38).

D. *Going About Doing Good*

With Chapter 3, Judd picked up again the story of Richard.
The boy found employment at the Green Mill saw mill, where,
before he was hired, he was subjected to a lengthy, tedious
Yankee discussion, designed to impress him with the necessity of
hard work at low beginning wages. There Richard, in a strange
place and among strange men, was introduced to Mr. Helskill,
the so-called Friend of the People. "I am the Friend of the
People," Helskill said in Richard's presence; "I look after the
public good; I vote for it at the polls; I canvass for it before
election . . .—my purse bleeds, and my heart bleeds, to see how
it is abused. . . . I am an advocate of the people; I defend their
rights; I teach them their independence; I stand between them
and monopoly; I take the brunt of oppression; I believe that men
are to be trusted,—that they *have* discretion" (54-55).

All this sounded good, but Richard soon saw Helskill for what
he was—one skilled in hellish ways—when Helskill urged
Richard to take a drink while on the job. "The laws of the mill
forbid drinking, and the laws of conscience forbid it" (57),
rejoined Richard. Declaring himself to be open-tongued,
Richard shouted at Helskill: "I will not inform against you
elsewhere; I will tell you to your face what you are, and what you
do. You bring mischief here; you bring fightings, ill-will, neglect
of work; you bring in sickness and disease; . . . you are
desperate in the business; you would send these men drunk from
the mill" (58-59). And when Helskill offered to give a lad a

drink, Richard dashed the bottle to bits with a handspike. Richard had weathered his first moral test.

Wishing to do good, Richard, soon after his encounter with Helskill, befriended an old grandfather and his sick and exhausted granddaughters. Richard asked Junia, one of the girls, if she had no friends in the city and if no clergyman had visited them. Richard read from the Bible and prayed with the old man and the girls and even succeeded in getting the old man acquitted on a charge of stealing.

E. *Formative Influences on Richard's Mind and Character*

In a chapter, simply entitled "Biographical," Judd told the story of the formation of Richard's mind and the development of his character. Like Judd, Richard was born in an interior town. As a boy, he fished and hunted and read books from the village library. Like Judd at Hadley, he studied philosophy, history, and Latin at the academy. Unlike Judd, Richard as a boy had an excellent clergyman who rambled the woods with the youths of the parish, introducing them to Nature and developing in them a sense of the beautiful. Pastor Harold—Judd sitting for his own portrait—taught also that

Christianity was designed to redeem mankind, and that the Church was a chosen instrument of this redemption. He sought to develop within the Church an Operative Philanthropy; and this principle he applied wherever it could subserve its great end. The evening religious meetings he divided into several sorts. In addition to what the Gospel could do for their souls, he urged it as a serious point upon his people, what it would make them do for others. In furtherance of this plan, different evenings were assigned to subjects: one to Intemperance; one to War; another to Slavery; a fourth to Poverty; and the enumeration went on till it comprised the entire routine of Practical Christianity. He called these meetings the Church Militant. . . . These meetings were of service to Richard; he gained thereby much valuable information, and was led to a clearer understanding, and a more vital impression of his duties and responsibilities. He had access to his Pastor's library, and in some sense to his heart; so that in many forms he shared largely in the renovating, spiritualizing and exalting influence, which this good man, from the pulpit, the fields, the evening meeting, and his study, shed over the town. (79–80)

Richard posted on the wall of his room the motto: "To Be

Good, and To Do Good." But realizing early in life that his forte
was physical rather than intellectual, Richard decided not to go
to college or enter one of the learned professions, "partly,
indeed, by reason of pecuniary impediments. He had no desire to
enter a store, and embark his all on the frail but exciting bottom
of commercial avocation. His ambition was to be a thorough and
upright mechanic" (80).

F. Clover: "Power Is Sweet; Might Is Glorious"

Richard's nemesis in the tale was a character by the name of
Clover. Most of the men at the mill were afraid of the Claggart-
like character, but Richard, like Billy Budd, was simply
inquisitive as to the secret of the man's power. Clover openly
proclaimed: "Enlargement, aggrandizement, glory, fame are
natural to the human breast; they are natural to my breast.
Power, might are honorable; and these I study to exercise—I do
something; I exercise power; I am ENLARGED" (100-101). To
Clover, lying was the viable means to power. "Did not our troops
tell, utter, manufacture, publish a hundred lies, in Mexico? Are
they to be taunted with lying? I am in Mexico; I am in enemy's
country, and I shall lie to further my victories. . . . Power is
sweet; might is glorious;—it gives a man reputation; it affords
him security; it protects him from assault" (101).

But when Clover made a menacing gesture with his fist toward
Richard, the lad said to the bully: "I would rather you should not
do that. . . . I should very much prefer that you would not repeat
it. I must respectfully request you to attempt it again in no form
whatsoever" (102). The matter was settled by a feat of strength
which Richard won, after which, perhaps to save face, Clover
bragged of his having cut Silver out with Miss Plumy Alicia Eyre.
"The most desirable woman falls to the most favored man,—that
is, to the strongest man. I am such a man and Silver is not" (105).

G. Doing More Good

Nothing or no one, however, kept Richard from doing good
when the occasion arose. He toured the city, saw the poverty in
Knuckle Lane, and wondered about the correlation between
poverty and meanness. He noted the contrast between the abode
of the Governor and his remarkable American family and the
homes of the poor and their squalor in Knuckle Lane. He
observed the sale of rum in the stores. And on one occasion,

when the Governor's horse was frightened by snow sliding from the rooftops, Richard seized the reins of the scared animal and probably saved the life of the Governor. Later, during a visit with the orphans at Whichcomb's, Richard was thanked by Melicent for his brave act. "I did not know who was in the sleigh" (135), replied the self-effacing lad.

H. *Phumbics: A Question of Cats and Dogs*

Chapter 10, entitled "A Chapter Respecting Which There Is a Doubt Whether It Ought to Be Introduced, N.B.—None But the Printer Obliged to Read It," is another of Judd's fanciful digressions. Claiming that the narrative of Richard "cannot proceed without allusion thereto" (146), Judd devoted the entire chapter to a Swiftean political satire. The whole matter, Judd said, was in a word, a question of cats and dogs—a matter of potentially terrible consequences and serious results. As Judd put it,

The origin of the dispute it is not easy to trace, but its principal elements are more readily deduced. Many years anterior to this tale, a respectable individual in Woodylin had his cat worried by a dog. Families were inflamed, neighborhoods took sides, and at last the whole city was drawn into the controversy. One party would have all the cats killed; the other denounced the dogs.

There was no harmony of purpose. Those who sought to destroy the dogs wished to preserve the cats; on the other hand, whoever was friendly to a dog became the determined enemy of a cat. Two parties were formed, and officered, and drilled, and propagated. The newspapers exposed one doctrine or the other; and when Richard came to the place, there were two dailies, discriminating according to the sentiment of the times. One of these was called The Catapult, a name borrowed from an ancient place of ordnance which was understood to have been employed against cats. The other bore the name of Dogbane; the sense of which is obvious. The people were sometimes called Dogs, or Cats, according to their respective preferences. The subject matter was ordinarily denominated "Phumbics." The origin of the term cannot be discovered. (146–47)

The effect of Phumbics was everywhere to be observed. Phumbical meetings were held; there were Phumbical reading rooms. Whenever the Dogbanians came into power, men with clubs pursued the objects of their fury, and the yelping of dogs

assaulted the ear; their blood coated the sidewalks; and their
carcasses covered the docks. A similar mania to kill occurred
when the Cat-killers assumed office. Both groups hated the
fence-men, whom they derided as whifflers, temporizers, and
trimmers. Even the course of trade was determined by
Phumbics. The Catapulters would transact business with
Catapulters; Dogbanians with Dogbanians.

To further compound the Phumbical problems, another
political group calling itself the Hydriatics or Water-men
appeared on the scene. The Hydriatics argued that "the
questions that had so long agitated the public mind were trifling
and useless,—that weightier issues should be considered. Their
doctrine was that more water should be used; that men ought to
be washed,—the city cleansed and purified" (149–150). The
Hydriatics even founded a party newspaper, the *Rinser*. Had the
older parties, however, united against the newer group, they
might have crushed it. Instead, they intensified their embittered
struggle against one another, while the Hydriatic interlopers
prospered, despite the propaganda bruited about that they were
intent upon introducing water into the city, thus setting the dogs
mad and filling the place with confusion and death.

The two older parties Judd was satirizing were no doubt the
Democrats and the Whigs. The Hydriatics, then, were the Free
Soilers, who rapidly emerged as a political power after the
founding of the party in 1848. Judd might have had in mind an
actual political struggle on the local level. But whether on the
local, state, or national level, Judd deplored political strife. A
little over two weeks after his ordination in Augusta, in the very
month that the nation received the outcome of the "hard cider"
election, and while Governor Fairfield of Maine, who attended
Judd's church awaited the results of a recount that would
ultimately spell defeat for him by less than one hundred votes,
Judd preached a sermon on August 18, 1840, on "Political
Strife."[4] Political parties "strike at the ties of human brother-
hood," he proclaimed. "All is fair in politics, though it be foul in
the market place," he continued. "The impeachment of motives
is a proclamation of hostilities. It is but a short step from the
State House to the Arsenal." Though Judd's sympathies were
with the Free Soilers and their desire to check the spread of
slavery, the spectre of the arsenal loomed ominously in the bitter

political struggle of 1848 that was being waged as Judd began his novel. He hated violence and division and the fighting like cats and dogs that internecine political struggle engendered.

I. *Doing Good Once More*

Judd picked up his episodic tale once more with Richard's going about doing good. He, for instance, physically restrained Clover from attacking a speaker who charged that the twin curses of war and slavery were cleaving like leprosy to the comeliness of the nation. He exhorted at a religious meeting, declaring that the world was one grand theatre for Christian usefulness. He visited the sick and attended a Sons of Temperance meeting in Quiet Arbor, a bar and gambling hall, where he proclaimed, "We come to-night to give you liberty. We proclaim your freedom. We have brought the Temperance Pledge" (214).

J. *A Talking River and a Talking Bridge*

But even before Richard found his way to the Quiet Arbor, Judd was off again down one of the naked paths in his narrative garden. In an episode likely suggested by the spring flood on the Kennebec in 1840 that burst the dam and damaged some of the property of his industrialist, land-speculating, and dam-building father-in-law, Judd treated his readers to a dialogue between a talking bridge and a talking river. The river overflowed, and the people feared the bridge would go, thus ruining the whole season's business. Peeved at the crassness of the people, the bridge complained that, year after year, it had enabled the people to cross the stream, only to receive, in turn, their ingratitude and scorn. "Shall I leap into the water?" the bridge asked. The river rejoined: "I know these fellows. . . . They thought they had me under their feet, when the ice was on, and they could cross for nothing. They thought I was of no consequence, and grudged the pennies they paid for getting over me. It was you, Mr. Bridge, that gave me a sense of my dignity and importance" (203–204). The bridge ordered the people to their knees, and the river fell when it was able to come to terms with the backbiters. Then later, in a chapter entitled "The June Freshet," Judd had a personified generalization, Man of Mind, warn of the weakness of the dam; but, in what may have been a bold slap at industrialists like his father-in-law, Judd had the mill and factory owners, in their selfish desire for water, scoff at the warning.

K. A Digression on Cities

More than halfway through his 468–page novel, Judd, at last, began to develop in earnest his central plot line, and only twice thereafter did he thrust lengthy digressions into the novel. One of these was his "A Tale may be like a garden" defense. The other—Chapter 29—is entitled "On Cities," a condemnation of one of the worst features of the mid-nineteenth-century big cities, but with a solution drawn directly out of More's *Utopia*. Judd apologized for breaking through "the proprieties of historical narrative" and, "after a hortatory sort" (321), presenting his arguments. But he was "moved" to attempt to account for the intemperance, licentiousness, beggary, disease, and theft that characterized the "preponderating and disproportionate vice of our cities" (321). The one cause was *Density*. Judd took N.P. Willis to task for reproaching the New Yorkers in his *Home Journal* for not being more willing to live several layers deep. As it was, Judd pointed out, they did not observe the Sabbath, but rather in the summer months took advantage of the day of rest to hie themselves off to Hoboken, Staten Island, or Brooklyn Heights for relief. Judd called for *Openness* through city planning that would assure that the streets would be at least four rods wide, that the churches would be conspicuous, that no more than two families would live under the same roof, and that parks, promenades, and trees would abound. The cities, Judd argued, need not be less populous, only more dispersed. There was land and enough for that. But what all this had to do with the sad conspiracy that was being hatched against poor Richard is a little difficult to see.

L. The Naive Lad and the Designing Female

The problem of the impressionable Richard was that he had come up against the amorous Miss Plumy Alicia Eyre and her designs, and he had trouble coping with the primeval temptation. The lad was struck by her dark, thrilling eyes, her pale, pensive, earnest face, and her searching, pleading, piteous heart. But, alas, hers was an unconverted mind that was not submissive to the orderings of Providence; thus she was bad and reckless. Yet she appealed to Richard's sympathies and thrilled every fiber within him. The wily girl knew, however, that she should not push the bewildered boy too hard and too fast. "Do not say that you love me; I do not wish you to say that. . . . Kiss me, and I go,—go with one assurance of friendship and happiness, which," she sighed, "if it be all that is allowed me, will be a precious keepsake forever" (266). Miss Eyre may well be Judd's most believably real character in the story.

Richard's emotional, amorously susceptible nature longed for Plumy Alicia; his reason, however, approved of Melicent, in whom he saw "purity without demureness, tenderness without insipidity, piety and no cant, beauty and no affectation, commonsense and yet great ardor and hope" (275). With Melicent, he could work happily among the down-and-outers in Knuckle Lane. "Into the full circle of his being she seemed to flow, and melt, and be as one with him; into his adoration of the Supreme, into his study of philanthropy, into his estimation of man, and all his consciousness of duty, she came" (329).

And as Judd increasingly warmed up to his story, he began to give the chapters suggestive titles: "The Undertow," "The 'Boil,' " and "Drawn Under." In "The Undertow," Miss Eyre, coming to realize she had lost Richard to Melicent, "matured a story that vitally touched his reputation" (337), claiming he had been attentive to her, confidential with her, and often alone with her. "He won my heart," she said. "I surrendered at discretion" (337). In "The 'Boil,' " Richard found it hard to believe Miss Eyre could have been so utterly abominable. The omniscient author informs the reader, however, that Miss Eyre was motivated by a wantonness of passion; and, like a cat with a mouse, she wanted to sport with her victim before putting him to death. Richard called on Miss Eyre; and in a bathetic, melodramatic style, Judd reported the encounter:

"Spare me this!" cried Richard, smiting his hand upon his brow. "Anything but such a thing! any torture you may inflict, but such a torture! Do not strew my path with the mutilated fragments of a heart! do not doom my vision to the sight of sensibility in ruins! Kill *me* in some other way!"

Miss Eyre leaned her hand upon the arm of her chair, and was heard to sob.

"Dear Plumy Alicia!" said Richard, approaching and attempting to take her hand. She waved him off.

"Go," said she; "your work is done, and mine is done!" (345)

Richard took himself heavily from the house. And in the chapter entitled "Drawn Under," he began to wonder wherein he had sinned.

M. *Being Good*

His compelling concern now was to know what God would have him do. His tedious soul-searching led him to the conclusion that, though he could no longer *do* good, he could *be* good. So he occasionally dropped in on Elder Jabson's evening meetings, and on one occasion explained "that the anticipated Coming of our Lord, so far as concerns this world, was a spiritual phenomenon;—that it was to be realized in the heart and life, and to be fulfilled in the amelioration of society and progress of the race" (374). He was spiritually refreshed by a vision of Jesus. He continued to aid the poor and to visit the sick in their bereavement and despair. All the while, he seemed to Melicent a model human being, despite Miss Eyre's charge against him.

N. *Richard, Clover, and the Underworkings of Providence*

Richard found out that the fiendish Clover was back of his problems, and he confronted him. Clover reiterated his theme:

"MIGHT IS RIGHT!! Might creates right,—sustains right,—is the sober little thing itself. This is the first principle of human affairs. It is the universal law. It is the method of the world; and I am the world. . . ."
"And you have interfered with my happiness?"
"You have insulted my banner! You have fished in my waters; you have interrupted my business; you have usurped authority in my domain; and I have crushed you!" (398)

In Chapter 39, in a short interlude that Judd entitles "In Which the Author Briefly Philosophizes on Man," Judd points to the solution of Richard's problem; for "let it be all solemnly said, there is an Underworking, as well as All-Encompassing God, who knits together the shattered fibres of existence, and repairs the breaches in the foundation of the soul" (400). Thus Richard, perhaps not aware of the underworking, went down into the country to seek out Junia, the granddaughter of the old man

Richard befriended soon after coming to Woodylin, hoping she
would be able to help him refute Miss Eyre's accusation, since
Junia had observed his guarded demeanor toward the aggressive
Plumy Alicia. Junia signed a paper clearing Richard, in so far as
she knew, of any ungentlemanly conduct. Richard then heard
that an associate of Clover's was willing to go to the Governor
and tell what he knew of the plot hatched by Clover and Miss
Eyre to ruin his reputation and thus his chances with Melicent.
Things were looking up for Richard.

Unexpectedly, Junia came to town; and in the very sentimental, melodramatic, and heartrending chapter that follows, Judd
pulled out all the stops. Junia visited the grave of her dead sister
Violet, and who—"like some penitent Spirit of Evil, meditating
among the vestiges of decay" (424)—should have been in the
cemetery but Miss Eyre. Miss Eyre followed Junia to the
Governor's, where Junia pled with Melicent to forgive Richard.
"I know him to be pure and good," she said. "And he loves you!"
(426). Junia admitted that she, too, loved Richard. She continued
in an emotional outburst reminiscent of the Brückmann-
Margaret-Jane story in *Margaret*:

> "Listen, oh best beloved of the best beloved! I love Richard;—I love
> him for his greatness and his purity; I love him with the instinct of
> girlhood,—I love him with the meditativeness of womanhood. I love
> you, oh precious sister of my soul! because you love him. I know what
> you feel; I share your sufferings. He too suffers. I have been near his
> heart; I have heard its lonely anguish; I have felt its tortured throbs. I
> love his happiness; and his happiness is your love; and the happiness of
> you both is your mutual reunion. I am his bride but through you. My
> love for him I give you. . . . And when, in the rapture of being, you can
> call him your own, remember, oh remember, that one, young and
> inexperienced,—too susceptible, perhaps too constant,—that Junia
> loved him too!" (427-28)

Miss Eyre had followed Junia; she overheard Junia's remarks to
Melicent, and even she was so touched that the wrong to Richard
could no longer go unrighted. Miss Eyre went to Melicent and
accused Mrs. Melbourne, a member of the Governor's household,
of encouraging her ambition to better herself, to rise from the
class into which she was born. "I saw Richard," she said. "—I
liked him;—I tell you I liked him! He united the loftiness of the

higher classes with the solid virtues of his own. I sprang toward
him, in my heart, wantonly wildly. . . . I intrigued,—yes, I was
trained to that. What selfishness of voluptuousness, what
shallowness of mediocrity, what cravings of the hod-clopper-
hood, have importuned for me, and sighed at my feet, and
cajoled my vanity!" (435-36). Miss Eyre believed she could make
Richard love her; but when she became convinced that this was
impossible, she, yielding to threats from Clover, allowed
untruths to be told and the false impressions of people to run
their course.

Richard and Melicent were married, and the Governor gave a
bridal party that was open to the public. The first and the last
families, the church people, the Friends of Improvement, the
Knuckle Laners, the Wild Olive boys in their whale jackets, and
the river drivers all came.

O. *The End of Clover*

At the beginning of Chapter 50, Judd announced that "without
book, bell or prayer, unshriven, unhousled, with no procession
and no sorrow, Clover died, and was buried" (452). According to
Judd, historic and prophetic justice required that he die. But it
would be difficult to imagine what requirements of narrative art
required the novelist to dispose of Clover in the way he did. The
end of Clover is a composite of a parody of the Congress in
Pandemonium in *Paradise Lost* and a situation drawn from
Chaucer's *The Pardoner's Tale*. Clover and his rowdies were
congregated in the Bay Horse Tavern on a night of pitch
darkness; gusts of wind smote the place; lightning flashed and
thunder rolled. Clover wanted action, but Weasand counseled,
"Let us be easy where we are, . . . and we can have a few more
pleasant rides before the Black Car comes along" (454). Carver,
who preferred the Bay Horse to his own parlor, echoed
Weasand. But Clover, in his cups, shouted, "O mighty thunderbolt . . . I AM THY FELLOW!" (454). He continued: "Compeer
of the Almighty, I, Clover, am;—the first and the last resort of
kings! I am lightnings!" (456). "I challenge," he said, "all the fires
of heaven! MEET ME, YE DREAD MINISTERS, WHERE YE
WILL—I AM READY!!" (457).

Clover decided he would meet the Dread Ministers at the Old
Oak in the Stone Pasture. There he would meet their Goliath,
the lightning. "I will tweak the nose of Vengeance! Come boys,—

FOLLOW ME!" (458). With that he seized his hat and rushed out with his companions following. At the Old Oak, Clover pounded his fist on the tree and, looking up, shouted, "Ye powers of heaven, or hell, I HAVE COME!!!" (458). Just then a flash of lightning struck him dead, and his comrades buried him where he fell. Clover found Death under the Old Oak like Chaucer's rioters.

P. *Parting Words*
Judd had now only to gather the loose ends of his story together and issue in Chapter 52 what he called the "Parting Words." Richard became an industrialist, built a fine house, got into politics like Senator Williams, and was elected mayor. Poor Miss Eyre, forgiven by others, could never forgive herself. But Judd chose not to end his tale with the mention of the fortunes of his characters. Rather he went off on several bizarre tangents, motivated, perhaps, by a sense of honesty and hope.

Judd realized that the perceptive reader would recognize in *Richard* many literary "borrowings," and to the authors of these works he wanted to express his thanks. With a touch of genial humor, he wrote: "If our publishers, who are obliging gentlemen, consent, we would like to forward a copy of the book to each of them. If they dislike any thing of theirs in this connection, they will of course withdraw it; should they chance to like any thing of ours, they have full permission to use it. This would seem to be fair" (464). Judd admitted, however, that, unlike Pope Gregory VII, who burned the works of Varro in order to keep St. Augustine from being charged with plagiarism, he would resort to no extreme measures to protect his fair name. In fact, he said, "It comports at once with manliness and humility to confess one's indebtedness" (465). And, after all, "plagiarism . . . is to be considered rather in the light of good cheer and kindly intercourse, than as evidence of meanness of disposition, or paucity of ideas" (465).

Q. *Literary Borrowings and the Novels of the Brontë Sisters*
Reference has already been made to Judd's indebtedness in his tale to Franklin, Swift, More, Milton, and Chaucer. The most obvious indebtedness, however, has not been mentioned—Judd's indebtedness to the novels of the Brontë sisters which appeared in 1847 and 1848. Plumy Alicia Eyre is more than suggested by

Charlotte Brontë's heroine. In many ways she is lifted bodily out
of one novel and dropped down in Woodylin. According to E. P.
Whipple, in an essay entitled "Novels of the Season" in the
October 1848 issue of the *North American Review,* "Not many
months ago, the New England States were visited by a distressing
mental epidemic, passing under the name of the 'Jane Eyre
fever,' which defied all the usual nostrums of the established
doctors of criticism. . . . The book which caused the distemper
would probably have been inoffensive, had not some sly
manufacturer of mischief hinted that it was a book which no
respectable man should bring into his family circle."[5] With the
"Jane Eyre fever" sweeping the area at the very time he began
to write *Richard,* Judd, it seems, decided to get on the
bandwagon, to capitalize on Charlotte Brontë's popular success;
and he made his most significant borrowing.

Clover, on the other hand, may well have been something of a
composite of the male villains in the sisters' 1847–48 novels.
Whipple in his essay refers to the profanity and brutality of the
misanthropic profligate Mr. Rochester and to the "torpedo
shocks to the nervous system" he causes in *Jane Eyre,* especially
when he is given to "the exhibition of mere animal appetite, and
to courtship after the manner of kangaroos and the heroes of
Dryden's plays."[6] Whipple was even more shocked by Heathcliff
in Emily's *Wuthering Heights,* whom he described as "a
deformed monster, whom the Mephistopheles of Goethe would
have nothing to say to, whom the Satan of Milton would consider
as an object of simple disgust."[7] He was the very epitome of
brutality, a creature disavowed by man and devil. And Gilbert
Markham in Anne's *The Tenant of Wildfell Hall,* says Whipple,
had "almost constantly by him a choice coterie of boon
companions, . . . and the reader is favored with exact accounts
of their drunken orgies, and with numerous scraps of their
profane conversations."[8]

R. *"Go, Little Book"*

Even after thanking the authors (whom he does not name) and
after declaring that "there is not probably a great author living
but that, like a certain great king, would gladly throw a chicken
or a chicken's wing from his feathered abundance to any poor
author, and enjoy its effect in lighting up the countenance of the
poor fellow's wife and children" (465), Judd still was not

through; he must, like Byron at the end of "Canto the First" of
Don Juan, bid his book farewell:

"VADE, LIBER,"
(GO, LITTLE BOOK,)

"Qualis, non ausim dicere, felix."
(What will be your fortune, I cannot tell.)

"Vade tamen quocunque lubet, quascunque per oras,
I blandas inter charites, mystamque saluta
Musarum quemvis, si tibi lector erit.
Rura colas, urbemque."

(Yet go wherever you like,—go everywhere,—go among kind people;
you may even venture to introduce yourself to the severer sort, if they
will admit you. Visit the city and the country.)

"Si criticus fector, tumidus censorque molestus,
Zoilus et Momus, si rabiosa cohors,"—approach,
"Fac fugias,"—fly.
"Laeto omnes accipe vultu,
Quos, quas, vel quales, inde vel unde viros."

(Look cheerfully upon all, men and women, and all of every condition.)
(466)

Judd bade his book go into the farmhouses, the workshops, and
the sordid abodes, there to teach young men how to rise in their
calling and to teach them that intelligence, industry, and virtue
are the only decent ways to honor and emolument. "And, more
especially, demonstrate to them, and to all, how they may BE
GOOD AND DO GOOD" (467).

Judd could not pass up the opportunity to relate *Richard* to
Margaret and *Philo:*

Should inquiries arise touching your parentage and connections,—a
natural and laudable curiosity, which, as a stranger in the world, you
will be expected to enlighten,—you may say that you are one of three,
believed to be a worthy family, comprising two brothers and one sister;
that, a few years since, your author published the history of a young
woman, entitled "Margaret, a Tale of the Real and the Ideal"; and that
at the same time, and as a sort of counterpart and sequel to this, he
embraced the design of writing the history of a young man, and you are

the result. The first shows what, in given circumstances, a woman can
do; the last indicates what may be expected of a man: the first is more
antique; the last, modern. Both are local in action, but diffuse in spirit.
In the meantime, he has written "Philo, an Evangeliad"; cosmopolitan,
ecumenical, sempiternal, in its scope; embodying ideas rather than
facts, and uniting times and places; and cast in the only form in which
such subjects could be disposed of,—the allegorical and symbolical; or,
as it is sometimes termed, the poetic. . . . "Philo" is as an angel of the
everlasting gospel; you and "Margaret," one in the shop, and the other
on the farm, are practical Christians. However different your sphere or
your manners, you may say you all originate, on the part of your author,
in a single desire to glorify God and bless his fellow-man. "Philo" has
been called prosy; "Margaret" was accounted tedious. You, "Richard,"
I know, will appear as well as you can, and be what you are,—honest
certainly, pleasing if possible. (467–478)

III   *Criticism*

Judd's narrative mélange may have been pleasing in the
farmhouses, workshops, and sordid abodes, if indeed it was read
in these places; but, like *Philo*, the critics largely ignored the
book. Only the *North American Review*, among the major
journals, chose to notice it at all. The author of the review—A.
W. Abbott—argued that, whatever else may be said of Judd, he
was no artist. In fact the tale, the title of which reminded him of
a voluble book peddler hawking his wares, is, he said, like
something whose growth is spontaneous, wildly luxuriant, but
wholly unpruned. Conceding that there is some beauty in the
tale, Abbott, however, found that "our sense of it is weakened
and disturbed by constant shocks and distractions, occasioned by
prevalent bad taste in style, and by many dramatic absurdities."[9]
Judd, he said, was guilty of using provincialisms in his own
vocabulary as author and of parading them in defiance of polite
usage; these are things no respectable writer would do,
whatever his theme or purpose. He also would not, as Judd had
done, leap from the sublime to the ridiculous, from high and far-
reaching thought to unmitigated silliness, and from "decent
scenes of sentimental comedy and oddly profane tragedy" to
"inimitable and exquisite . . . absurdity."[10] To Abbott, only
Munk, Roxy, and their children—not Miss Eyre—were excellent
portraitures. "When we leave the threshold of Munk and Roxy,"
he wrote, "we leave consistency behind. From the heaps of

outlines, among which the shadows fad as if the light were purposely thrown from a many-sided reflector, the coloring imagination brings out figures much like those in Punch, with wonderfully big heads, making speeches that were never concocted by any human brain, and uttering words the meaning and derivation of which not even a slang dictionary could expound."[11] Abbott objected also to the "pseudo-republicanism"of the novel and to "the catastrophe, which borrows the thunderbolt as a special interposition of Divine vengeance upon this 'embodiment of horridness.' "[12] The use of the *deus ex machina* to dispose of Clover was revolting not only to Abbott's taste, but to his religious sentiments as well. But despite all, Abbott still thought the author of *Margaret*—yes, even the author of *Richard*—had as yet not realized his potential as a writer.

So far as we know, Judd did not write any letters of explanation concerning *Richard* to the Reverend Edward Everett Hale, nor did he make any pleas to editors that they temper their reviews, using as their guideline the morality of criticism. Judd may well have decided that with *Richard* he would write a novel to suit himself, perhaps aware that his novel of sentiment, as he wrote it, was unlikely to please the critics. And perhaps he little cared whether or not he pleased the critics. Even if they charged it with vulgarity—as he could have guessed they would—he knew that his was a serious book designed to benefit man and glorify God. Even if the novel lacked artistic unity—as Judd admitted it does—it still, he felt, had a unity born of the author's heart and purpose.

No doubt Judd knew that *Richard* was not as good a novel as *Margaret,* and he must have known why. By setting *Richard* in the Augusta of his own day, he forfeited the romantic aura that historical distance provided in *Margaret. Richard* too lacked the rich folklore of the earlier story, as well as its archaic flavor and the racy folk idiom of the rural Yankee patois. While in both novels Judd's shortcomings as a storyteller are apparent, the theme of *Margaret* guided and somewhat controlled the narrative. The theme of *Richard*—Richard's being good and doing good—encouraged an episodic development of the plot and made Judd believe—perhaps half seriously—that artistically he could justify his many digressions on the basis of his "garden" theory of the tale and his argument that a tale, like life it purports to depict, should not follow an ordered progression. But of more moment from an artistic standpoint is the fact that *Richard* did not provide Judd with the occasion, except perhaps in the case of the snowstorm with which the novel opened, to demonstrate his skill in nature description as he was able to do in *Margaret*. And Judd needed something to soften the heavy-handed didacticism of his tale more than the literary borrowings and the story of bruited seduction could provide. No second edition was demanded of *Richard Edney and the Governor's Family*. And, alas, no translations were made so that our Usbek relatives and Ottoman friends might become acquainted with a worthy family of the United States of North America.

CHAPTER 6

The White Hills, An American Tragedy

I *The Preparation: In Search of Local Color*

WELL before *Richard Edney and the Governor's Family* came off the press, Judd was planning another work. This one—a drama—Judd planned to set in the White Mountains of northern New Hampshire. As a series of small notebooks or diaries among the Judd Papers at Harvard show,[1] Judd made trip after trip into the White Mountains to acquaint himself with the scenery and the local color of the area. For instance, on August 11, 1850, Judd in one of the diaries recorded his impressions of Lake George, of the "shadow of the mountain by moonlight on the lake," and of the sight of "the steamer John Jay in the white mist." From Lake George, he traveled to Littleton and Franconia; and in an entry for August 23, Judd mentioned some of the folklore of the area, the night spent on Mt. Washington, and the splendor of the peak of the mountain at sunrise. The next autumn, as his "The White Hills" diary for September 1851 indicates, he was back in the mountains recording descriptions of mountain plants, a mountain thunderstorm, the "remarkable vapor," recording the story of a man lost in the hills, and so on. And on October 10, 1851, as a stitched "White Mountain" diary shows, he was in Gorham, N.H., noting the peculiarities of the scenery. He marveled at "the mists creeping along the valley at night, low horizontal, [with] the moon above them." He found the "blue shadows reflected in Bryant's Pond beautiful" and delighted in the "silvery appearance of the hills at Shelbourne." Judd apparently started work on his manuscript—"The White

Hills, An American Tragedy"—in September 1851, as a
manuscript note indicates, and virtually completed a rough draft
sometime in the next year. However, the portion of the play
published by Miss Hall in her *Life and Character of the Rev.
Sylvester Judd* seems to break off somewhat abruptly, and a
cryptic note by Miss Hall would seem to indicate that Judd died
before completing his manuscript in final form.[2]

II *"The Mania of Owning Things"*

We have no idea what Judd's plans for publication might have
been. At his death, the unpublished manuscript, along with other
Judd papers, went to Miss Hall, who published selections from
the blank verse drama, interspersed with some prose summaries.
The five-act closet drama deals allegorically with the mania for
wealth and riches. According to Miss Hall, "the basis of the idea
was suggested by the general rage for California gold, which, for
a year or two before its commencement, had been so rife
amongst most all classes of the community."[3] Like Thoreau, Judd
believed all this added up to a clear case of national immorality.
Judd, like Thoreau, chose to locate the seat of covetousness in
the human heart.

In a note on the first page of the manuscript, Judd indicated
that his drama "contains an allusion" to a passage in James
Sullivan's *The History of the District of Maine* (1795). Sullivan
had declared that Columbus, when he discovered the New
World, was not in search of gold but that, as soon as "the mines of
Mexico and Peru were opened, the Europeans changed their
taste for chivalry and conquest, to a more violent propensity for
the obtaining of wealth by fortuitous events: and, therefore, the
first adventurers to the northern part of the continent, paid their
attention principally to that object."[4] In fact, so Sullivan said, the
naturally sagacious North American Indians, discovering the
Europeans' passion for gold, encouraged the adventurers in their
fruitless pursuit by telling them of mountains of ore which never
existed and of the riches that could be theirs in the interior of the
country.

III *The Legend of the Great Carbuncle*

There followed in Sullivan's account a passage which Judd
copied on the first page of his manuscript:

The White Mountains have a singular appearance, when viewed from a distance: their tops are white like snow. There was an early expectation of finding a gem, of immense size and value, on this mountain: it was conjectured, and it is yet believed by some, that a carbuncle is suspended from a rock over a pond of water there. While many, in the early days of the country's settlement, believed this report, each one was afraid that his neighbor should become the fortunate proprietor of the prize, by right of prior possession. To prevent this, credit was given to the tale of the natives, that the place was guarded by an evil spirit, who troubled the waters, and raised a dark mist, on the approach of human footsteps.[5]

Judd found the legend of the suspended carbuncle suitable to his dramatic purpose in *The White Hills, An American Tragedy* just as Hawthorne had earlier found it suitable to his narrative purpose in "The Great Carbuncle, A Mystery of the White Mountains."

Judd may well have picked up also from Sullivan the idea of the witches and the Faustian motif of his drama. In those early days, according to Sullivan, "visions, dreams, witchcraft, and familiar spirits, were every where talked of"; and in their inclination to believe dreamers and soothsayers who claimed to know where treasures could be found, "many innocent persons fell victims to the delusion, under an accusation of their having entered into special covenants with the devil, and having derived miraculous powers from him."[6]

IV *The Drama*

A. *Normand's Obsession and the Pact with Mammon*

As with *Richard,* Judd set the scene for his final creative effort in the America of his day. The principal character, Normand, was one who made the acquisition of riches the motivation of his actions until the end of act four; he was, until then, willing to hazard soul and body in his obsessive pursuit. Like the young Judd, Normand, a promising student, suffered in his soul the curse and sting of pinching poverty. It was not that Normand valued wealth for its own sake; he wanted rather the gratifications, the respect, and the consideration that he was convinced wealth alone would bring:

> Alas! I'm poor. What is it to
> Be poor? Is it to lack bread, credit, smiles,

> Attendance? To be hungry, cold? 'Tis not
> To want, but not to be. 'Tis that one's wants
> Become one's being, and his hates his master.
> 'Tis to feel mean, before some meaner clay
> That one would spit upon. 'Tis not to suffer,
> But to be pitied; it is not to need,
> But not to dare to ask. 'Tis not that men
> Neglect me: it is that I shrink from them,
> Abjure the sun, and hide me from the street,
> And hesitate at gentle courtesies
> Of woman. This is to be poor. I could
> Endure, defy perdition, kiss despair;
> But let me be respected. With a proud
> And lofty mind, I'm no man's peer; down, down,
> Abject, dependent. I am not a slave:
> I wish I were. I hate the poor: of all
> That God hath made, they are the vilest thing.[7]

While Normand bemoaned his penury, Mammon, in the guise of a man of the world, entered, learned of Normand's maddening thoughts, and led him to a place where they could view the White Hills in the distance. Mammon waved a magic wand, handed Normand a spyglass, and bade him see the immense and radiant gem. Normand determined to seize the prize, but he was warned by Mammon of the danger that awaited him from the guarding genius and of the futility of attempting to snatch the gem in his then unprepared condition. Thus, Mammon called up the witch Vafer to aid the determined lad. Normand was told he must give up Leirion, the girl he loved, and the cross he wore as a symbol of his faith. In his wild excitement and in order to gratify his overmastering passion, Normand was willing to surrender all that meant most to him. Faust-like, he entered into a compact with Mammon, selling his soul to the god of riches.

But soon a sobering reaction set in, accompanied by frightful misgivings, the loss of inward peace, and the remembrance of his innocent childhood, his blind mother's prayers, and the pious life of his dead brother:

> Was it some spiritual trance, a scene evoked
> In fever's fitful change, or history
> Of natural things? Bright to the uttermost,
> It weighs on me like gloomy death, or sigh

Disastrous, 'splendent death, auroral grave,
Down which, with all my better life, I plunged.
Reflection, like a tempest, sweeps my heart
Of every trace of pleasure; sadness reigns.
. . . .
What am I? Changed from what I was, or such
Self-questioning had never passed these lips.
Conscience is dead, stone dead; the bent and aim
I cherished of a higher good in life,
More consonant with virture, of deserved
Renown, and benefit to human kind
If living, burns like a forgotten lamp.[8]

But he was determined:

I will be rich: I'll have estates,
A seal, blood, quality, and living;
Some right of way along this crowded world;
The smiles of art, and thanks of charity.
Had I the means, I'd do extensive good
As any man. I'll rise, and so un-god
The age, and purge this odium from man.[9]

Normand visited Leirion, who sensed that Normand was
greatly troubled. When she found out about Normand's fear of
poverty, she said, "We will be poor together"[10]; but Normand
argued that he could not bring the "bitter load" to her:

Leirion.
We shall be free
With moderate desires, rich from content,
And passing happy in each other's love.
Normand.
Whence fertile ease, illustrious action whence,
The charms of culture, or e'en nature's joy?
Leirion.
From our good souls, love, worth a mint a year.[11]

B. *Normand and Vafer, the Witch-Mother*

Normand rejected the prayful pleas of Leirion and went to
keep his rendezvous with Vafer, the witch-mother. Normand was
told that, before he took on the guardian giant and the dangers of

the lake, he must secure his mother's blessing on his quest, secure a miser's curse and put it in a bag, find a cat in which a dead man's soul resided, go to a "feted beer-shop" and get a drunkard's penny, gather a sprig of sorrel from his brother's grave, and so on. Then, in addition, Normand must marry the ugly and vile Turpis, the daughter of Vafer, at the wedding of which the deathlike Pernix and the bony Sklerote, relatives of Vafer, would "groom the festive scene."

Normand fulfilled Vafer's preliminary conditions and went to the abode of the witches in a cavern on a small wooded island in Lake George, ready to marry Turpis. But before Simon Magus could marry them, a luminous shadow of Leirion bearing a cross appeared and caused the witch-party to vanish, thus foreshadowing the vanishing of Vafer at the end of act four. This, of course, was Judd's way of saying in his allegory that Normand was not yet beyond redemption, indeed, never would be.

The farther Judd got into his drama, the more fanciful became the adventures of his hero. Finally wedded to Turpis, equipped with the proper witch charms, and sure now that the gem was his for the taking, Normand set out on his perilous journey, accompanied by Vafer, metamorphosed now as a raven. As the unlikely pair went on their way, Vafer tried to keep Normand from resting on the steps of a church, but he drove the bird away. Inside, the people were singing:

> Return, my roving heart, return,
> And chase these shadowy forms no more;
> Look out some solitude to mourn,
> And thy forsaken God implore.[12]

The preacher then preached from the text "What if you gain the world, and lose your soul." As Normand left the church steps, a procession of fairies, bearing a dead soul, crossed his path, chanting a dirge which he regarded as an obsequy for his own soul.

C. *"And Chase These Shadowy Forms No More"*

The song, the sermon, and the chant reminded Normand once again of his spiritual danger. This time he heeded the warning; in humility of spirit he turned back to the All-Forgiving God; and Vafer's hold over him vanished. In act five, Normand, under the

influence of the beauties of nature and his consciousness of the
God of nature, was gradually restored to a balanced attitude
toward life, nature, and God. Normand did not give up his search
for the gem, but he came to see the gem in its proper
perspective, as something of value but not something for which a
man should jeopardize his immortal soul. Judd was not taking a
position against the pursuit of wealth, only against the obsessive
pursuit that would cause a man to sell his soul to Mammon.

At the beginning of act five, Normand, alone at night in the
White Hills, gazed at the towering peaks and said:

> How still the mountains! as if God were all
> In all; whose calm and bright beneficence,
> Doth so englory soul and place, and shade
> And height, as we were in eternity,
> And sight were bliss, and consciousness a worship.[13]

But despite his awareness of the presence of the Almighty in
nature, Normand had not yet come to a proper appreciation of
the superior worth of nature as over against the inferior and
limited value of material things. It was the mountain guide that
Normand engaged at the Saco Notch and with whom he
traversed the hills who helped Normand get his values straight.
Normand quizzed the guide concerning any knowledge he might
have of the legend of the fabulous gem and offered to buy from
the guide his mountain lands. The guide replied:

> In all these haunts
> And pleasant things, yield me the right of way,
> I should not mind who held the fee. Like trees,
> We are rooted beings, growing to our birthplace.
> I've roamed these woods, and clambered every height,
> The roe-buck tamed, and wrestled with the lynx;
> . . . .
> I wake with cascades for my morning psalm;
> My sleep is soothed with murmuring forest-winds;
> And thunder, terrible beyond conceit
> Of lowland dwellers, is my Sunday organ.
>   Normand.
> Shades of Bach! What effect! These ancient towers,
> And long-drawn aisles, and tinted lights, with such
> A pipe to roll cathedral harmonies!

> To worship here some summer afternoon,
> With maidens holy in the solemn underwood,
> Their hands together pressed, and on their hair
> A glory from the saintly fountain streaming,
> And on their silver cross—Go on, good friend;
> I hang upon thy words as on a brink.[14]

In the dialogue that followed, the guide told Normand of the wandering, bodiless, lost men in the ravines—apparently men who lost body and soul in fruitless quests for the gem.

Near the end of scene four of act five, Normand came upon an undiscovered lake, nestled in the sides of the mountain. How far he had come in his appreciation of nature is revealed in his apostrophe to the lake:

> Sable and glassy wave, where swan-fleets ride,
> The beryl goblet of the monarch-bird,
> Where cougar's harbor and bittern shrieks,
> Untouched by sunbeam and by storms o'erpassed!
> O Mountain Tarn! the pure and amber glass,
> In secret chambers, dim and holy, where
> Daughter of God, ideal Beauty, fits
> And renovates immortal radiance,
> Whenas she visits the fond dreams of youth,—
> A sumptuous drop from nectared urns of heaven,—
> I drink of it.[15]

In the fifth scene of act five—perhaps the scene with which Judd intended to bring his play to a conclusion, but also perhaps not—Normand talked with his friend the artist. Now confident of his own grasp of nature, Normand felt free to instruct others as to how they could fully appreciate nature's charms and powers. The artist followed his advice. Walking away from him, Normand said: "The dread resolve of grandeur stirs within,/Nor medium flights shall tempt his vigor more."[16] These lines with their Miltonic echoes were apparently the final lines of the manuscript. Miss Hall commented: "Here fell the author's pen; his hand—*was stilled.*"[17]

V   *No "Medium Flight"*

Judd's play, of course, is not a tragedy in any strictly classical or modern sense. In Judd's view, it was, no doubt, a representation or presentation of a serious action—a work approaching a mode of tragicomedy of the sort developed by Beaumont and Fletcher in which the romantic plot employs love, treachery, and intrigue, but which ends with a melodramatic reversal of fortune for the protagonist who had hitherto been headed for disaster. This is not to say—or even to imply—that Judd consciously followed any model in the writing of his play. We simply do not know. He may well have trusted his moral consciousness to suggest the poetic treatment. Here was the minister-poet at work; of that we may be sure.

But in *The White Hills* we do note a marked development over *Philo* in Judd's ability to handle blank verse, to bend the lines to his purpose and to make them flow. Perhaps, as in the case of his artist in *The White Hills*, he felt the "dread resolve of grandeur stir within," and he determined that no "medium flights" would "tempt his vigor more." In fact, had Judd lived and had he continued to write—as all indications are he would have—he may well have realized most fully in dramatic poetry the promise the reviewers were wont to claim to be his.

CHAPTER 7

Coda

I *The Nineteenth-Century Critics*

IN the two decades following Judd's death in 1853, the critics who commented on his work were virtually unanimous in declaring Judd's forte as a novelist to lie in his unusual knack in depicting the New England character and the New England scene. When Arethusa Hall's *Life and Character of the Rev. Sylvester Judd* appeared in 1854, both the *Christian Examiner* and the *North American Review* published lengthy reviews. Edward Everett Hale in the *Examiner* praised Judd as one who showed himself "a most efficient philanthropist, a practical, working minister," but also one who "gradually achieved, at the same time, a much wider reputation, as the author who has best understood the New England character and best portrayed it in its nice details."[1] Apropos of *Margaret*, Hale admitted, however, that some of the enthusiasm with which it was received could be accounted for because the critics were seeking for "a real piece of 'American Literature.' "[2] J. H. Morison in the January 1855 issue of the *North American Review* declared that "no American writer surpasses Mr. Judd, we know of no one who equals him, in the lifelike delineation, or rather the fresh creation, of natural scenery and events. . . . No one, not even Mr. Emerson, has led us through such snow-storms as are made to visit us in 'Margaret' and 'Richard Edney.' "[3] According to Morison, Judd's "characters have a clearly defined individuality. . . . They live so in the heart of nature, that it sometimes is difficult to say whether they are a part of the landscape, or the landscape a portion of their being."[4]

The publication in 1856 of Felix O. C. Darley's *Compositions in Outline . . . from Judd's Margaret* provided—at least ostensibly—the occasion for Samuel Osgood to write a lengthy, rambling article for the April 1857 issue of the *North American Review* entitled "The Real and the Ideal in New England." Osgood found Judd to be in the mainstream of New England life, a partaker of the heritage and legacy of Dr. Channing, Webster, Prescott, Motley, and Bryant. As Osgood put it, "New England people are certainly remarkable for their love of beautiful scenery,"[5] and from almost every page of Judd's *Margaret* the author's love of nature "bursts out . . . like wild flowers from a rich prairie."[6] Judd gave us, Osgood said, "a rich and suggestive picture of the new life then budding out from the old stock."[7] But, alas, Judd was not *the* American novelist the devout were waiting for. However, Osgood wrote, Judd "has performed his task so well that we cannot but wish for the coming of a novelist who shall unite his spontaneous freshness with broader philosophic and more exact historic portraitures."[8]

The publication in 1866 of George Eliot's *Felix Holt* may have been the immediate impetus for an article in the July 1867 issue of *Fraser's Magazine,* perhaps the only and surely the fullest treatment of Judd's work ever to appear in a British journal. The anonymous critic said that Richard Edney is a New England Felix Holt; indeed, he continued, "the similarity of his character and many of the incidents of the story to those of *Felix Holt* is curious, all the more so because of the many internal evidences that they are coincidences."[9] The writer of the article—one who "saw and listened to Mr. Judd about a year before his death, when he was pleading before the autumnal assembly of Unitarian ministers for the general adoption in their churches of the principle that children should be regarded as members of them by birthright, and that they should take care to have their faith associated in every child's mind with its innocent gaieties"[10]—drew heavily upon Miss Hall's work, but he also had before him as he wrote Judd's creative works, and he quoted lengthy passages from *Margaret, Philo,* and *Richard Edney.* The purpose of the article seems to have been to show that Judd was "born under the old *régime*—that out of which the Unitarian movement sprang by a recoil,"[11] that like many another cultivated young man he passed in stages to Unitarianism, but that, like the unjustly maligned Parkerites and Transcendentalists, he went beyond the colorless form of Unitarianism of Dr. Channing. Judd's creative works, then, were his efforts to set forth in a pleasing artistic way his response to the spiritual demands of his day. The critic was careful to avoid labeling Judd a Transcendentalist, but the implication is there.

In fact, most of the critical attention devoted to Judd since the *Fraser's* article—as little as it has been—has been designed to identify Judd, in one way or another, with the Transcendental movement. The most oft-repeated assertion along this line is the summarylike statement by Octavius Brooks Frothingham found on the last two pages of his *Transcendentalism in New England: A History*, first published in 1876. After admitting that well-known writers of romances owed little to Transcendentalism and that indeed one had little right to expect of Irving, Paulding, or Cooper an interest "in ideas so grave and earnest," Frothingham said of Judd's *Margaret*: "A very remarkable book in the department of fiction was Sylvester Judd's 'Margaret; a tale of the Real and the Ideal; Blight and Bloom.' It contains the material for half a dozen ordinary novels; was full of imagination, aromatic, poetical, picturesque, tender, and in the dress of fiction set forth the whole gospel of Transcendentalism, in religion, politics, reform, social ethics, personal character, professional and private life."[12] Nowhere else, however, in his study did Frothingham mention Judd; nevertheless, the reader may likely conclude from Frothingham's one statement that Judd was to be regarded as a Transcendentalist in very good standing.

However, Frothingham likely would have had the same difficulty in labeling Judd specifically that he had in labeling Dr. William Ellery Channing specifically—and for the same reasons. For instance, Frothingham admitted that the splendid things Dr. Channing said "about the dignity of human nature, the divinity of the soul, the moral kinship with Christ, the inspiration of the moral sentiment, the power of moral intuition, habitual and characteristic as they were, scarcely justify the ascription to him of sympathy with philosophical idealism. His tenacious adherence to the record of miracles as attesting the mission of Christ, and his constant exaltation of the Christ above humanity, suggest that the first principles of the transcendental philosophy had not been distinctly accepted, even if they were distinctly apprehended."[13] Channing, as Frothingham pointed out, accepted the dogma that Christ was preexistent in the family of Heaven before his coming into the world, that he came to execute the most sublime purposes of his Father, that he ever lives as the Mediator, Intercessor, Lord, and Savior of mankind, and that "He is through all time, now as well as formerly, the active and efficient friend of the human race."[14] Thus Frothingham was forced to conclude that Dr. Channing was "not a Transcendentalist in philosophy." Dr. Channing's position was Judd's position.

In 1840—two years before his death—Dr. Channing, speaking of Transcendentalism, said that "in its opinions generally I see nothing to give me hope. I am somewhat disappointed that this new movement is to do so little for the spiritual regeneration of society."[15] And the next year, Dr. Channing in a letter to James Martineau said that the Transcendentalists were "in danger of substituting private inspiration for Christianity."[16] This also was Judd's position. The best Frothingham could conclude then was that Dr. Channing "was a Transcendentalist in feeling." No doubt Judd, too, was a Transcendentalist *in feeling*—however one may interpret the term. No doubt he shared with the most ardent of the Transcendentalists and indeed with Emerson some of their most cherished views, but they were views that his particular kind of liberal Christianity with its several unique features, his Christology, his view of the church as a vital and necessary spiritual and social institution, and his concept of the Christian ministry dictated. He was no man's disciple. His one recorded meeting with Emerson, for instance, was characterized by cold acrimony.[17] Indeed, his works portray Judd as a man who was never content to violate his own nature; his works were creative attempts to extend his own ministry and to make some reasoned statements about the great issues as he saw them. And his works should be approached accordingly.

II *Judd and Twentieth-Century Criticism*

Most of the critical attention devoted to Judd in the twentieth century unfortunately has had as its purpose to argue that Judd was an Emersonian. Philip Judd Brockway in his *Sylvester Judd: Novelist of Transcendentalism* (1941)—the only study of Judd approaching full length since Miss Hall's compilation—maintains that Judd derived his greatest inspiration from the ideals of Emerson's Transcendental philosophy. Indeed, Brockway argues that, in order to analyze the contributions of Judd, one must "show his relation and acquaintance with the Transcendental movement, especially its leader, Emerson, and the influences such relationship may have had upon the development of his thinking."[18] Brockway even asserts that *no* adequate study of Judd's writing—especially *Margaret*—can be made that does not "show Judd's portrayal of Emersonian and Transcendental ideals."[19] Yet Brockway admits that beyond *Margaret* such a study would run into difficulty. He cannot himself find Emerson in *Richard Edney*—"The medium is changed,"[20] he says—and, speaking of Judd's alleged Emersonianism, Brockway admits that Judd seemed in his second novel to have "lost the heart of that dream."[21] But even before that, by the time Judd was writing *Philo*, says Brockway, "Transcendentalism, for him, had begun to exhaust its inspiration; perhaps . . . the 'fount ran dry' and the earlier enthusiasm with which he embraced the philosophies of the Transcendentalists had begun to exhaust itself."[22] Brockway's study, therefore, illustrates the dangers and the difficulties of attempting to transplant the works of one author into the ideological body of another. The danger is that the transplant may be rejected as incompatible. Judd's brand of Transcendentalism should be mined from his works without preconceptions.

III   *Summing Up*

Judd is thought of today—when he is thought of at all—as a man of one book, as the author of *Margaret*. And perhaps rightly. It was and is a significant contribution to American letters, not because Judd demonstrated in *Margaret* that he was a first-rate storyteller—for he did not and was not—but because with *Margaret* he awakened anew the possibility of a fiction distinctively American. He demonstrated the obvious possibility of using effectively native American settings and scenery in narrative literature. He demonstrated the appeal of folklore, the richness of native American speech and dialect,[23] and the romantic appeal to Americans of their historical past. But despite his rather auspicious entry on the American literary scene, Judd did not realize in his later creative works the promise earlier critics had recognized. Nevertheless, Sylvester Judd merits a more prominent place in the history of American letters than has hitherto been allowed him.

Notes and References

Preface

1. *The Poetical Works of James Russell Lowell* (Boston, 1897), p. 145.

2. Quoted in Franklin B. Sanborn, "Letters. By Henry Thoreau," rev. of *Letters to Various Persons*, ed. Ralph Waldo Emerson, Boston *Commonwealth*, August 12, 1865.

3. *The Writings of Margaret Fuller*, ed. Mason Wade (New York, 1941), p. 370. On October 5, 1846, Margaret Fuller wrote Alexander Ireland (MS., Princeton University Library) that Judd had written her because "he wished me to know that I had one admirer in the State of Maine, a distinction of which I am not a little proud, now that I have read his book." The letter, misdated October 6, is quoted in Moncure D. Conway, *Autobiography, Memories and Experiences of Moncure Daniel Conway* (Boston, 1904), I, 179.

4. *The Journals and Miscellaneous Notebooks of Ralph Waldo Emerson*, ed. Ralph H. Orth and Alfred R. Ferguson (14 vols. to date [1979]; Cambridge, 1971), IX, 381.

5. Arethusa Hall, "Sathurea: The Story of a Life," pp. 38–39. MS., Judd Papers (55M-1), Houghton Library, Harvard University.

6. See *Memorabilia from the Journals of Sylvester Judd of Northampton, Mass., 1809–1860*, ed. Arethusa Hall. Private edition (Northampton, Mass., 1882), *passim*.

7. "Autobiography" in *Arethusa Hall: A Memorial*, ed. Francis Ellingwood Abbott. Privately printed for the family (Cambridge, 1892), pp. 57–58.

8. *Life and Character of the Rev. Sylvester Judd.* Compiled by Arethusa Hall (Boston, 1854), p. vi.

9. Ibid., p. vii.

Chapter One

1. *Life and Character of the Rev. Sylvester Judd*, p. 463.

2. Jonathan Edwards's sermon, when printed, was entitled *The Great Concern of a Watchman for Souls, Appearing in the Duty He Has to Do, and the Account He Has to Give, Represented & Improved, In a*

143

Sermon Preached at the Ordination of the Reverend Mr. Jonathan Judd, To the Pastoral Office Over the Church of Christ, in the New Precinct at Northampton, June 8, 1743 (Boston, 1743).

3. *Life and Character of the Rev. Sylvester Judd*, p. 7.

4. *Memorabilia from the Journals of Sylvester Judd of Northampton, 1809-1860*, pp. 20-21.

5. Ibid., p. 23.

6. Ibid., p. 39.

7. Ibid., p. 42.

8. Ibid., pp. 44-45.

9. Ibid., p. 48.

10. Ibid., pp. 54-55.

11. Ibid., p. 55.

12. The elder Judd's account of his trip is found in Sylvester Judd II, "Journal of a Trip to Ohio," Judd Papers (55M-1), Houghton Library, Harvard University.

13. *Memorabilia from the Journals of Sylvester Judd of Northampton, 1809-1860*, p. 43.

14. Ibid., pp. 58-59.

15. Ibid., p. 61.

16. [Sylvester Judd], *A Young Man's Account of His Conversion from Calvinism. A Statement of Facts.* Printed for the American Unitarian Association. 1st Series. No. 128 (Boston, 1838), pp. 4-5.

17. Ibid., p. 5.

18. *Life and Character of the Rev. Sylvester Judd*, pp. 23-24. See also *Memorabilia*, p. 45, for what the elder Judd had actually written: "I do not remember of building any airy castles respecting riches since my boyish days. Indeed, so *ardent* has been my desire for knowledge, and so sluggish my desire for the accumulation of property, that I feel convinced that I ought to have been sent to college in my earlier days; not because I should have been a great scholar, but because I should have been in employment congenial with my feelings. But the time has passed, and cannot be recalled."

19. Ibid., pp. 29-30.

20. Ibid., p. 32.

21. Ibid., p. 34.

22. Ibid., p. 39.

23. Ibid., pp. 42-43.

24. Ibid., pp. 49-50.

25. Ibid., p. 63.

26. Ibid., p. 64.

27. *Memorabilia from the Journals of Sylvester Judd of Northampton, 1809-1860*, p. 89.

28. Ibid., p. 90.

29. Ibid.

30. See "Biographical Notes" by A[rethusa] H[all] in Sylvester Judd [the elder], *History of Hadley, Including the Early History of Hatfield, South Hadley, Amherst, and Granby, Massachusetts, with Family Genealogies by Lucius M. Boltwood* (Northampton, Mass., 1863), p. 6.

31. Among the Judd Papers in the Miscellaneous Manuscripts Collection of the Library of Congress are ten letters written in late 1835 or early 1836 by such men as Samuel J. May and others to the elder Judd concerning various antislavery activities in the Northampton area.

32. *Life and Character of the Rev. Sylvester Judd*, p. 75.

33. Ibid., p. 76.

34. Ibid., p. 77.

35. Ibid., p. 78.

36. Ibid.

37. Ibid., p. 80.

38. Ibid., p. 82.

39. Ibid., p. 84.

40. Ibid.

41. Ibid., p. 92.

42. Ibid., pp. 98–99.

43. *Emerson's Complete Works* (The Harvard Edition, 6 vols., Boston, 1929), II, 115.

44. *Life and Character of the Rev. Sylvester Judd*, p. 116. Italics mine.

45. *Emerson's Complete Works*, II, 85.

46. *Life and Character of the Rev. Sylvester Judd*, pp. 116–17.

47. *Emerson's Complete Works*, II, 95.

48. *Life and Character of the Rev. Sylvester Judd*, p. 123.

49. *The Early Lectures of Ralph Waldo Emerson, 1836–1838*, ed. Stephen Whicher et al. (3 vols., Cambridge, 1964), II, 309.

50. Ibid., II, 355.

51. *Life and Character of the Rev. Sylvester Judd*, pp. 146–47.

52. "The New Birth" was first published in the *Salem* (Mass.) *Observer*, October 27, 1838.

53. MS., Judd Papers (55M-2) Houghton Library, Harvard University.

54. Edwin Gittleman, *Jones Very: The Effective Years, 1833–1840* (New York, 1967), p. 163. Other biographical information about Very is taken from Gittleman, *passim.*

55. *Life and Character of the Rev. Sylvester Judd*, pp. 134–35.

56. Ibid., p. 136.

57. See the poem "Beauty" in Jones Very, *Essays and Poems* (Boston, 1839), p. 122. Although beauty is *only* from the fountain that is Divine, Very admits that he almost loved beauty better than God.

58. *Life and Character of the Rev. Sylvester Judd*, p. 141.

59. MS., Judd Papers (55M-1), Houghton Library, Harvard University.

60. *Life and Character of the Rev. Sylvester Judd*, p. 345.

61. Ibid.

62. Ibid., p. 346. Italics mine.

63. *A Young Man's Account of His Conversion From Calvinism*, p. 29.

64. *Life and Character of the Rev. Sylvester Judd*, pp. 171-72.

Chapter Two

1. *Life and Character of the Rev. Sylvester Judd*, p. 175.

2. Ibid., p. 188.

3. Ibid., p. 232.

4. Ibid., p. 275.

5. Sylvester Judd, *The Beautiful Zion: A Sermon* (Augusta, 1841), p. 22. See footnote number 1, Chapter Three.

6. Ibid., pp. 22-23.

7. *A Moral Review of the Revolutionary War, Or Some of the Evils of that Event Considered. A Discourse Delivered at the Unitarian Church, Augusta, Sabbath Evening, March 13th, 1842. With an Introductory Address, and Notes* (Hallowell, Maine, 1842), p. [3].

8. Ibid.

9. Ibid., p. 43.

10. Ibid., p. 47.

11. *Life and Character of the Rev. Sylvester Judd*, p. 195.

12. Samuel J. May, Letter to Sylvester Judd, 10 May 1842, Judd Papers (55M-2), Houghton Library, Harvard University.

13. *Life and Character of the Rev. Sylvester Judd*, p. 198.

14. Ibid., p. 201.

15. Ibid., p. 209.

16. *Arethusa Hall: A Memorial*, p. 42. *The Works of William E. Channing* was published in six volumes in 1846. Three of Emerson's works were published before 1846: *Nature* (1836), *Essays: First Series* (1841), and *Essays: Second Series* (1844).

17. Ibid., p. 47. The book by Carlyle that Miss Hall was probably referring to was his *German Romance: Specimens of Its Chief Authors* (Boston, 1841).

18. Ibid., pp. 52-53. Carlyle's translation of *Wilhelm Meister's Apprenticeship* in three volumes was published in Edinburgh and London in 1824 and in Boston in 1828. An English translation of *Goethe's Correspondence with a Child* in three volumes was issued in London, 1837-1839. E. H. Noel's translation of Richter's *Flower, Fruit, and Thorn Pieces; or the Married Life, Death, and Wedding of the Advocate of the Poor, Firmian Stanislaus Siebenkas* was published in

Boston by Munroe in 1841. *The Vestiges of the Natural History of Creation* by Robert Chambers was published in London in 1844. The full title of Andrew Jackson Davis's book is *The Principles of Nature, Her Divine Revelations, and a Voice to Mankind* (New York, 1847). In 1842, James Munroe and Company published *The Miscellaneous Writings of Theodore Parker.*

19. Ibid., p. 79.
20. Ibid., p. 96.
21. Ibid., p. 97.
22. *Life and Character of the Rev. Sylvester Judd,* p. 278.
23. Ibid., p. 280.
24. Ibid., p. 281.
25. Ibid., pp. 281–82.
26. Ibid., p. 284.
27. *The True Dignity of Politics: A Sermon by the Rev. Sylvester Judd, Preached in Christ Church, Augusta, May 26, 1850* (Augusta, Maine, 1850), n.p.
28. Ibid., p. 3.
29. Ibid., p. 8.
30. Ibid., p. 21.
31. *Life and Character of the Rev. Sylvester Judd,* pp. 239–40.
32. Ibid., p. 250.
33. Reverend Sylvester Judd, *The Church in a Series of Discourses* (Boston, 1854), p. 103.
34. Ibid., p. 20.
35. *The Birthright Church: A Discourse by the Late Rev. Sylvester Judd, of Augusta, Maine* (Augusta, 1854), pp. 28–29.
36. *Life and Character of the Rev. Sylvester Judd,* p. 293.
37. Ibid., p. 294.
38. Ibid., p. 307.
39. Ibid., p. 308.
40. Ibid., pp. 310–11.
41. Ibid., p. 311.
42. Rev. Sylvester Judd, *A Discourse Touching the Causes and Remedies of Intemperance. Preached February 2, 1845* (Augusta, 1845), p. 37.
43. Ibid., pp. 14–15.
44. Ibid., p. 21.
45. Ibid., p. 27. Judd is here quoting from what he called "certain sentiments" of Dr. William Ellery Channing.
46. *Life and Character of the Rev. Sylvester Judd,* p. 319.
47. Ibid., pp. 319–20.
48. Ibid., p. 300.
49. Ibid.
50. Ibid., p. 301.

51. Ibid., p. 303.
52. Ibid., p. 415.
53. Ibid., p. 417.
54. Ibid., p. 418.
55. Ibid.
56. Ibid., p. 419.
57. Ibid., p. 419–20.
58. Ibid., p. 420.
59. "The Dramatic Element in the Bible," *Atlantic Monthly* IV (August 1859): 138.
60. Ibid., p. 139.
61. Ibid., p. 146.
62. Ibid., p. 153.

Chapter Three

1. It is interesting also to note that the kind of Christian social order advocated in *The Beautiful Zion* anticipated almost exactly the aims and structure of the Christian social order developed on Mons Christi in *Margaret.* "My thoughts," Judd said, "are engaged this morning, with contemplations upon The Beautiful Zion. I would describe some of the characteristics of the Good Society" (p. 5). The Good Society would be made up of a group of people that God had chosen as a special people. "He has *separated us from all the people of the earth to be his inheritance*" (p. 6). "From our holy hill we shall commiserate the world; while we look out upon it, we shall labor to reflect the beauty of our situation through the thickest of its darkness, and earnestly pray for the hour when the *law shall go forth out of Zion, and the word of the Lord from Jerusalem* (p. 9). There "science, poetry and the arts would shed a grace upon the daily walks of our religious life" (p. 11), and there the children would be educated "in a manner corresponding with their natures" (p. 12). Christian love for one another would characterize the society, resulting in harmony among the people and the banishment of flagrant vice. ". . . The dwellers on the holy mountain will be remarked for their support of the principles, and adherence to the practice of *social rectitude*" (p. 17). Judd concluded: "Then shall our Zion *be beautiful for situation, the joy of the whole earth*" (27).

2. *Life and Character of the Rev. Sylvester Judd,* p. 350.

3. In its Judd Manuscript Collection, the Forbes Library of Northampton has sixty-four bound volumes of the elder Judd's manuscripts, each volume containing approximately 300 pages. The material is uncatalogued. However, the following titles of a few of the volumes will indicate some of the elder Judd's interests that might have been of interest to Sylvester as he was planning *Margaret:* "Revolutionary Matters," "Miscellaneous and Indians," "Hampshire Matters,"

"Natural History," "Miscellaneous, Old Houses, Old Meeting-Houses," and five volumes entitled "Chronology and History."

4. *Life and Character of the Rev. Sylvester Judd*, p. 350.

5. The first manuscript chapter of *Margaret* and the last manuscript chapter of *Margaret* are among the Judd Papers (55M-2) in the Houghton Library of Harvard University.

6. *Life and Character of the Rev. Sylvester Judd*, p. 205.

7. Sylvester Judd, Letter to James Munroe, 23 November 1844, the Barrett Collection of the University of Virginia Library.

8. James Munroe, Draft of a letter to Sylvester Judd [25 November 1844], the Barrett Collection of the University of Virginia Library.

9. Sylvester Judd, Letter to James Munroe, 23 March 1845 (Ch.B5.47), the Boston Public Library; and Sylvester Judd, Letter to James Munroe, 1 April 1845 (Ch. B5.49), the Boston Public Library.

10. James Walker Judd was a partner in the Hartford firm of Andrus & Judd, book printers, binders, and sellers. By "publish," Judd likely meant "print." See *Memorabilia from the Journal of Sylvester Judd of Northampton, 1809-1860*, pp. 72-73.

11. Hannah More (1745-1833) was a prolific writer of poems, plays, and polemics. Her most widely reprinted moral work was called *Practical Piety; or, The Influence of the Religion of the Heart on the Conduct of Life*. The works of Mrs. Charlotte Elizabeth Browne Phelan Tonna (1790-1846), with an introduction by Harriett Beecher Stowe, were published in three volumes in 1843 by the American Sunday-School Union. In 1833, the American Tract Society published *The Child at Home; or, The Principle of Filial Duty* by John Stevens Cabot Abbott (1805-1877); and in 1835, the American Tract Society published *The Young Christian; or, A Familiar Illustration of the Principles of Christian Duty* by Jacob Abbott (1803-1879).

12. *Life and Character of the Rev. Sylvester Judd*, pp. 353-55.

13. *A Young Man's Account of His Conversion from Calvinism*, p. 21.

14. Sylvester Judd, *Margaret. A Tale of the Real and the Ideal, Blight and Bloom* (1851; rpt. Upper Saddle River, N.J., 1968), pp. 3-4. This is a reprinting of the 1871 Roberts Brothers' edition of *Margaret*, a one-volume edition of Judd's two-volume revised edition, published in 1851 by Phillips and Sampson. The 1968 reprint of *Margaret* by the Gregg Press is, unless otherwise noted, cited because of its general availability to the modern reader. Subsequent page references are cited parenthetically in the text.

15. All quotations from the newspapers and journals cited in this paragraph were taken from the clippings in the notebook, Judd Papers (55M-2), Houghton Library.

16. [F. D. Huntington], rev. of *Margaret. A Tale of the Real and Ideal*, . . . , *Christian Examiner* XXXIX (November 1845): 418.

17. Ibid.

18. Ibid., p. 419.

19. Ibid.

20. Ibid., p. 420.

21. [W. B. O. Peabody], rev. of *Margaret; A Tale of the Real and Ideal,* . . . , *North American Review* LXII (January 1846): 102.

22. Ibid., p. 103.

23. Ibid., p. 106.

24. Ibid., p. 107.

25. Ibid., p. 110.

26. Ibid.

27. Ibid., p. 116.

28. [Dexter Clapp], rev. of *Margaret; A Tale of The Real and Ideal, Blight and Bloom;* . . . , *Southern Quarterly Review* IX (April 1846): 507.

29. Ibid.

30. Ibid., p. 509.

31. Ibid., p. 511.

32. Ibid., p. 517.

33. *The Works of Orestes A. Brownson,* collected and arranged by Henry F. Brownson (20 vols. New York, 1966), VI, 113.

34. Ibid., VI, 114.

35. Ibid.

36. Ibid., p. 115.

37. *The Writings of Margaret Fuller,* ed. Mason Wade (New York, 1941), p. 370.

38. [James Russell Lowell], rev. of *Kavanagh: A Tale,* by Henry Wadsworth Longfellow, *North American Review* LXIX (July 1849): 209.

39. Ibid., pp. 209–10.

40. [Sylvester Judd], *Margaret. A Tale of the Real and Ideal, Blight and Bloom; Including Sketches of a Place Not Before Described called Mons Christi* (Boston, 1845), pp. 40–41.

41. Ibid., p. 54.

42. Ibid., pp. 66–67.

43. Sylvester Judd, Letter to [F. O. C. Darley], 31 December 1851, Special Collections, The University of Iowa Library.

Chapter Four

1. Deborah M. Taft, Letter to Sylvester Judd, 28 December 1845, Judd Papers (55M-2), Houghton Library, Harvard University.

2. Sacvan Bercovith, *The Puritan Origins of the American Self* (New Haven, 1975), p. 143.

3. The Millerites were members of the Adventist Church led by William Miller (1782–1849), who predicted in 1831 the end of the world and Christ's second coming in 1843.

4. *Life and Character of the Rev. Sylvester Judd*, p. 367.

5. Ibid.

6. Ibid., p. 406.

7. Ibid., p. 365.

8. Ibid., p. 364.

9. Jones Very, *Essays and Poems* (Boston, 1839), p. 3.

10. Ibid., p. 5.

11. Ibid., p. 7.

12. Ibid., p. 22.

13. [Sylvester Judd], *Philo: An Evangeliad. By the Author of 'Margaret; A Tale of the Real and Ideal'* (Boston, 1850), pp. 7–8. Subsequent page references are cited parenthetically in the text.

14. *Life and Character of the Rev. Sylvester Judd*, p. 368.

15. Ibid., p. 365.

16. Ibid., p. 366.

17. Ibid., p. 368–69.

18. Sylvester Judd, Letter to Henry W. Bellows, 24 March 1850, Massachusetts Historical Society.

19. [A. P. Peabody], rev. of *Philo: An Evangeliad. By the Author of Margaret; A Tale of the Real and Ideal*, *North American Review* LXX (April 1850): 434.

20. Ibid., p. 440.

Chapter Five

1. [Sylvester Judd], *Richard Edney and the Governor's Family. A Rus-Urban Tale, Simple and Popular, Yet Cultured and Noble, of Morals, Sentiment, and Life Practically Treated and Pleasantly Illustrated containing, also, Hints on Being Good and Doing Good* (Boston, 1850), p. 467. Subsequent page references are cited parenthetically in the text.

2. Sylvester Judd, Letter to his father, 16 February 1841, Judd Papers (55M-1), Houghton Library, Harvard University.

3. Richard D. Hathaway, "The Lapse of Uriel: The Conversions of Sylvester Judd (1813–1853)," Diss. Western Reserve, 1964, p. 359.

4. The sermon in MS. is in the Judd Papers (55M-2), Houghton Library, Harvard University.

5. [E. P. Whipple], "Novels of the Season," *North American Review* LXVII (October 1848): 355.

6. Ibid., p. 356.

7. Ibid., p. 358.

8. Ibid., p. 359.

9. [A. W. Abbott], rev. of *Richard Edney and the Governor's Family; . . .* , *North American Review* LXXII (April 1851): 494.

10. Ibid., p. 496.

11. Ibid., p. 498.

12. Ibid., p. 499.

Chapter Six

1. The Judd Papers (55M-2), Houghton Library, Harvard University.

2. See also "Sylvester Judd," *Fraser's Magazine* LXXVI (July 1867): 59. The anonymous author of the article who seems to have known Judd personally wrote of *The White Hills:* "As he was writing the last scene of this work the curtain fell upon it, and upon many other high hopes and aims—the curtain of death."

3. *Life and Character of the Rev. Sylvester Judd,* p. 377.

4. James Sullivan, *The History of the District of Maine* (Boston, 1795), p. 74.

5. Ibid., pp. 74–75.

6. Ibid., p. 75.

7. *Life and Character of the Rev. Sylvester Judd,* p. 379.

8. Ibid., pp. 381–82.

9. Ibid., p. 382.

10. Ibid., p. 385.

11. Ibid., pp. 385–86.

12. Ibid., p. 394.

13. Ibid., p. 396.

14. Ibid., p. 398.

15. Ibid., p. 399.

16. Ibid., p. 400.

17. Ibid.

Chapter Seven

1. E[dward] E[verett] H[ale], rev. of *Life and Character of the Rev. Sylvester Judd, Christian Examiner* LVIII (January 1855): 63.

2. Ibid., p. 74.

3. [J. H. Morison], rev. of *Life and Character of the Rev. Sylvester Judd, North American Review* LXXX (April 1855): 428.

4. Ibid., p. 431.

5. [Samuel Osgood], "The Real and Ideal in New England," *North American Review* LXXXIV (April 1857): 544.

6. Ibid., p. 545.

7. Ibid., p. 550.

8. Ibid., p. 551.

9. "Sylvester Judd," *Fraser's Magazine* LXXVI (July 1867): 56.

10. Ibid., p. 60.

11. Ibid., p. 46.

12. Octavius Brooks Frothingham, *Transcendentalism in New England: A History* (New York, 1876), pp. 382–83.

13. Ibid., pp. 110–11.

14. Ibid., p. 111.

15. Ibid., p. 112.

16. Ibid.

17. *Journals of Ralph Waldo Emerson*, ed. E. W. Emerson and Waldo Emerson Forbes (10 vols., Boston, 1912), VIII, 290. Emerson noted in his journal: "I saw Judd in Augusta, in February [1852], and asked him who his companions were? He said, 'sunsets.' I told him, I thought they needed men. He said, 'He was a priest and conversed with the sick and dying.' I told him, Yes, very well, if people were sick and died to any purpose; but, as far as I had observed, they were quite as frivolous as the rest, and that a man peremptorily needed now and then a reasonable word or two."

18. Philip Judd Brockway, *Sylvester Judd (1813–1853): Novelist of Transcendentalism* (Orono, Maine, 1941), p. xii.

19. Ibid.

20. Ibid., p. 85.

21. Ibid., p. 92.

22. Ibid., p. 100.

23. For instance, I have counted eighty-five words in John Russell Bartlett, *Dictionary of Americanisms A Glossary of Words and Phrases, Usually Regarded as Peculiar to the United States* (New York, 1848) that list *Margaret* as the first printed source. A partial list follows: *to bouge* (to swell), *dadducks* (rotten bodies of trees), *to inheaven* ("a word invented by the Boston transcendentalists"), *pung* (rude sort of sleigh), *pimping* (little, pretty), *pesky* (great), *pupelo* (cider-brandy), *scranch* (crunch), *to see how the cat jumps* (to discover secrets), *to skink* (to serve drink), *snip-snap* (tart dialogue), *to trig a wheel* (to stop a wheel to keep it from going backwards), *tongs* (pantaloons), *strippings* (last and richest milk drawn from a cow), *a staddle* (a young tree left to grow where others are cut), *to wheal* (to swell).

Selected Bibliography

The major depository of Judd manuscripts and documents is the Houghton Library of Harvard University. The uncatalogued Judd Papers are stored in eighteen boxes. Two boxes of papers (55M-1)—containing letters by various members of the Judd family, other personal papers, a journal of a trip to Ohio by the elder Judd, and such manuscripts as Arethusa Hall's "Sathurea: The Story of a Life"—were donated to the Houghton Library by Mrs. Sylvester Judd Beach. The remaining sixteen boxes (55M-2)—containing holograph letters, notes, student papers, plays in manuscript, manuscript poems, a scrapbook of clippings of reviews, etc., the first and last chapters of the manuscript of *Margaret*, a hundred or more neatly stitched handwritten sermons, a number of pocket diaries, newspapers containing reports of Judd's preaching and lecturing, and books from Judd's library—were deposited in the Houghton Library by the Kennebec Historical Society of Augusta, Maine.

In addition to the uncatalogued manuscripts and documents, Harvard University has two Judd letters, fMS Am 1603 (169a) and Ac 8. J8854. Zz8519. The other Judd manuscripts are scattered. Columbia University has two Judd holograph letters in its Sydney Howard Gay Collection—one to the *Anti-Slavery Standard* and the other apparently to Sydney Howard Gay. The Chicago Historical Society has one letter, dated November 27, 1852, from Judd to an unknown addressee concerning a lecture. The New York Historical Society has one early letter, dated July 30, 1838, about a trip Judd was planning to take to Hartford. The Historical Society of Pennsylvania has a Judd letter, dated January 29, 1852, to an unnamed fellow minister about exchanging pulpits. The University of Iowa has one letter—Judd's reply to Darley's request. Four Judd letters are in the Barrett Collection of the University of Virginia. There is one letter, dated January 29, 1850, in the Fessenden Papers of the Maine Historical Society in which Judd offers the Augusta Unitarian Church to the Maine Peace Convention for a meeting. Two letters from Judd to James Munroe concerning the publication of *Margaret* (Ch. B5.47 and Ch. B5.49) are in the Boston Public Library. The letter from Judd to Henry W. Bellows is in the collection of the Massachusetts Historical Society. And Yale University has a manuscript—probably in Arethusa Hall's hand—of Judd's lecture on "The Dramatic Element in the Bible."

154

PRIMARY SOURCES

Judd's Works (in order of publication)

"What is Truth?" *Yale Literary Magazine* I (June 1836): 129–31. A brief essay that argues the inadequacy of language as a means of setting forth truth to the extent that "Many points lie equally balanced between truth and falsehood."

"The Outlaw and His Daughter." *Yale Literary Magazine* I (June 1836): 155–61. A tale of stilted prose and no dialogue but reminiscent of *Margaret* in situation and scene. The daughter of an outlaw, grows up beside a lake in New England, where pond and girl are kindred and where the honorable suitor gains the hand of the "Bird of the Lake."

A Young Man's Account of His Conversion From Calvinism. A Statement of Facts. Printed for the American Unitarian Association. 1st Series. No. 128. Boston: James Munroe & Co., March 1838. Four letters addressed to "Dear W——n."

The Little Coat: A Sermon. No. 9 [Cincinnati: American Reform Tract and Book Society, *ca.* 1840]. Reprinted in the Unitarian Sunday-School Society's Tract Series, No. 14, n.d.

The Beautiful Zion. A Sermon Preached July 4, 1841. Augusta, Maine: Severance and Dorr, Printers, 1841.

A Moral Review of the Revolutionary War, Or Some of the Evils of That Event Considered. A Discourse Delivered at the Unitarian Church, Augusta, Sabbath Evening, March 13th, 1842. With An Introductory Address, and Notes. Hallowell: Glazier, Masters & Smith, Printers, 1842.

A Discourse Touching the Causes and Remedies of Intemperance. Preached February 2, 1845. Augusta: William T. Johnson, Printer, 1845.

Margaret. A Tale of the Real and Ideal, Blight and Bloom; Including Sketches of a Place Not Before Described, Called Mons Christi. Boston: Jordan and Wiley, 1845.

"Worth of the Soul." In *Sermons on Christian Communion, Designed to Promote the Growth of the Religious Affections, by Living Ministers.* Ed. T. R. Sullivan. Boston: William Crosby and H. P. Nichols, 1848, pp. [24]–37.

Philo: An Evangeliad. By the Author of 'Margaret: A Tale of the Real and Ideal.' Boston: Phillips, Sampson and Company, 1850. Reissued in 1852.

The True Dignity of Politics. A Sermon . . . Preached in Christ Church, Augusta, May 26, 1850. Augusta: William T. Johnson, Printer to the State, 1850.

Richard Edney and the Governor's Family. A Rus-Urban Tale, Simple

and Popular, Yet Cultured and Noble, Of Morals, Sentiment, and
Life, Practically Treated and Pleasantly Illustrated . . . By the
Author of "Margaret," and "Philo." Boston: Phillips, Sampson and
Company, 1850. Roberts Brothers of Boston reprinted Richard
Edney in 1880.

Margaret: A Tale of the Real and the Ideal . . . Revised Edition . . . by
the Author of "Philo." Two volumes. Boston: Phillips, Sampson and
Company, 1851. Volume one has 391 pages; volume two, 304.
Phillips and Sampson brought out a reprinting of the two-volume
revised edition in 1857. In 1871, Roberts Brothers of Boston
published a new one-volume edition of the revised version with
401 pages and issued reprints in 1882 and 1891. In 1968, Gregg
Press reprinted the Robertses' one-volume edition.

The Birthright Church: A Discourse by the Late Rev. Sylvester Judd
. . . Designed for "Thursday Lecture" in Boston, Jan. 6, 1853. Ed.
Joseph H. Williams. Boston: Crosby, Nichols, and Company, 1853.
The work, with an altered title, was reprinted in Augusta by W. H.
Simpson in 1854 for the Association of the Unitarian Church of
Maine.

The Church: In a Series of Discourses. Ed. Joseph H. Williams. Boston:
Crosby, Nichols, and Company, 1854. The volume of sermons was
reprinted by the Boston publisher D. C. Colesworthy in 1857.

"The Dramatic Element in the Bible." Atlantic Monthly IV (August
1859): [137]-53.

SECONDARY SOURCES

ANON. "Sylvester Judd." Fraser Magazine LXXVI (July 1867): [45]-60.
Most lengthy article on Judd ever published in a British journal.
Though it draws heavily on Miss Hall's biography, it was written by
one who knew Judd personally. The writer, quoting freely from
Judd's creative works, seems to want to respond to a question
ascribed to Carlyle: "What great human soul has it [New England]
produced?"

Arethusa Hall: A Memorial. Privately printed for the family and edited
by Francis Ellingwood Abbott. Cambridge: John Wilson and Son,
1892. Publishes Miss Hall's reminiscences of Sylvester's spiritual
struggles, her "Autobiography," and extracts from her private
notebooks and journals.

BERCOVITCH, SACVAN. The Puritan Origin of the American Self. New
Haven: Yale University Press, 1975. Finds a startling similarity
between Judd's Theopolis Americana in Margaret and Cotton
Mather's Theopolis Americana.

BROCKWAY, PHILIP JUDD. Sylvester Judd (1813-1853): Novelist of Transcendentalism. Univerity of Maine Studies, Second Series, No. 53,

published in the *Maine Bulletin* XLIII (April 1941): No. 12. Orono,
Maine: University of Maine Press, 1941. Argues that Judd "was the
one definite novelist of Transcendentalism," that his first novel
demonstrates that he was indeed an Emersonian, but that Judd
soured on Transcendentalism after writing *Margaret.*

———. "Sylvester Judd: Novelist of Transcendentalism." *New England
Quarterly* XIII (December 1840): 654–77. Deals only with
Margaret, the philosophy of which, "it seems certain, grew directly
from the basic principles of Emersonian Transcendentalism," and
thus "stands as a unique expression in our literature of the ideals of
the great leader of New England thought, translated by a
contemporary into the pages of fiction."

BROOKS, VAN WYCK. *The Flowering of New England, 1815–1865.* New
York: E. P. Dutton & Co., 1937. Finds that *Margaret* is a Utopian
romance, a Fourieristic fantasy drawn largely from Goethe's
Wilhelm Meister, and an argument for Messianic socialism, yet
some of its scenes are so vividly picturesque as to rival the best
scenes of Hawthorne.

CLARK, HARRY HAYDEN. *Transitions in American Literary History.*
Durham: Duke University Press, 1953. Quotes Moncure D.
Conway as saying that he found revealed in *Margaret* the whole
spiritual history of New England. According to Clark, Judd was the
only one among those regarded as Transcendentalists, hampered as
they were by their faith in intuition as the source for inspiration,
who had the ability and interest to work out the complex symbols
required in the structure of the novel.

CUTLER, B. P. *A Sermon Preached at Park Street Church, Portland,*
[Maine], *Sunday, Jan. 30, 1853 . . . Occasioned by the Death of
Rev. Sylvester Judd.* Portland: H. J. Little & Co., 1853. Reprinted
in the *Monthly Religious Magazine* VIII (1853): 125–37. Deals
principally with Judd's work as a minister, yet he "was a man of the
present age. He looked forward and not back."

DUYCKINCK, EVERT A. and GEORGE L. *Cyclopaedia of American
Literature.* 2 vols. Philadelphia: William Rutter Co., 1875. A short
sketch of Judd's life drawn from Miss Hall's biography and the
reprinting of a New England snow scene from *Margaret.* Judd
received about the same space in the work as Theodore Parker,
Thoreau, Melville, and E. E. Hale.

FROTHINGHAM, OCTAVIUS BROOKS. *Transcendentalism in New England: A
History.* New York: G. P. Putnam's Sons, 1876. Frothingham
declares *Margaret* to contain the material for a half-dozen ordinary
novels and to set forth "in the dress of fiction . . . the whole gospel
of Transcendentalism in religion, politics, reform, social ethics,"
and so on.

HALL, ARETHUSA. "Sathurea: The Story of a Life." MS., Judd Papers

(55M-1), Houghton Library, Harvard University. Especially help-
ful in providing a picture of the home life Judd knew as a boy.
HATHAWAY, RICHARD D. "The Lapse of Uriel: The Conversions of
Sylvester Judd (1813-1853)." Diss. Western Reserve, 1964. This is
the best study to date of the intellectual milieu Judd came out of.
Hathaway says Judd was converted from Calvinism to a conserva-
tive Transcendentalism *only temporarily*. After *Margaret*, he
rejected Transcendentalism and "accepted limitation."
HUTCHISON, WILLIAM R. *The Transcendentalist Ministers: Church Reform
in the New England Renaissance*. New Haven: Yale University
Press, 1959. Judd is regarded as an early Transcendentalist.
KING, DONALD R. "Emerson's 'Divinity School Address' and Judd's
Margaret." *Emerson Society Quarterly* XLVII (1973): 3-7. Argues
that it is more than a coincidence that an outline of Emerson's
"Divinity School Address" and the narrative plan of *Margaret* are
so similar.
Life and Character of the Rev. Sylvester Judd. Compiled by Arethusa
Hall. Boston: Crosby, Nichols, and Company; New York: C. S.
Francis and Co., 1854. Reprinted in 1857 by D. C. Colesworthy and
in 1971 by Kennikat Press. The beginning point in any study of
Judd. In her 531-page biography—Miss Hall preferred to call it a
compilation—she published the Judd manuscripts, letters, and
journals she had carefully collected, obviously with Judd's
cooperation.
LOOMIS, C. GRANT. "Sylvester Judd's New England Lore." *Journal of
American Folklore* LX (April/June 1947): 151-58. An excellent
study of Judd's memorable scenes, the narrative use of folklore,
and his native idioms in *Margaret*.
*Memorabilia from the Journals of Sylvester Judd of Northampton,
Mass., 1809-1860*. Ed. Arethusa Hall. Private edition. Northampton, Mass.: Metcalf and Co., Printers, 1882.
VAN DOREN, CARL. *The American Novel, 1789-1939*. New York:
Macmillan Company, 1949. Written to show that Unitarians could
produce imaginative literature, *Margaret* is nevertheless badly
constructed, drifts into a region of misty transcendentalisms, but
has genuine merits in its depiction of New England scenes.

Index

159